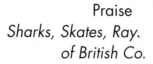

Praise
Sharks, Skates, Ray.
of British Co. ...

The more we come to know about and appreciate the lives
of some of our lesser-known sea creatures, the better we,
as a society, can protect their—and our—future. Kudos to
Gordon and Jackie for the considerable time, effort and
expertise that go into generating such a publication, and to
Andy's photographic vision that brings the species to life.
The smart use of "Quick Bite" references allows us a glimpse
of the importance of these species to local First Nations and
provides the reader with meaningful local coastal connections.
I thoroughly enjoyed the opportunity to read this and realize it
will be valuable to researchers, commercial fishermen and the
public—especially children.

> —W.E. Lorne Clayton, executive director,
> Canadian Highly Migratory Species Foundation, and
> co-owner, IEC International

Sharks, Skates, Rays and Chimeras of British Columbia is an
indispensable guide to an incredible and misunderstood
group of animals. In addition to being a guidebook that will
introduce BC residents to the many fascinating species that live
in or visit our waters, this book contains an introduction to key
scientific and conservation principles associated with sharks
and their relatives. Full of great information and beautiful
photographs, this book is a must-have for marine biologists
and fish lovers alike!

> —Dr. David Shiffman, marine conservation biologist,
> former Simon Fraser University Liber Ero Postdoctoral
> Research Fellow

Who knew that there could be so many different sharks, skates, rays and chimeras in BC waters! This eye-opening handbook and field guide, which combines amazing photographs and insightful species information, provides just the type of information most valued by divers, naturalists, commercial and sport fishers, fish biologists and managers, or indeed anyone interested in marine life. Sharks, skates and their relatives are truly fascinating creatures, and this handbook highlights their diversity off the west coast of Canada.

—Dr. Steven E. Campana, professor of fisheries, Faculty of Life and Environmental Sciences, University of Iceland

Detailed, thorough, comprehensive and wonderfully illustrated. This compendium of up-to-date information on sharks, skates, rays and chimeras of British Columbia is authored by well-known and respected scientists with a wealth of personal experiences and expertise. The background biological information is easily understandable, the treatment of each species provides a guide to understanding the unexpectedly wide and surprising diversity of this group of animals in Canadian waters, and the exceptional photographs by Andy Murch make this a standout addition to any library for scientists and non-scientists alike.

—Dr. Jeffrey C. Carrier, professor emeritus of biology, Albion College, and senior editor of *Biology of Sharks and Their Relatives*

The authors have assembled an impressive compendium. After spending a lifetime at sea commercial fishing, I find this book provides valuable insight for ecological and fisheries scientists, managers and resource harvesters to consider when assessing how best to conserve and sustain these important species. The authors' contributions to this subject reflect years of experience and dedication to improving our understanding of and relationship with aquatic ecosystems.

—Brian Mose, executive director, Deep Sea Trawlers Association

Sharks, Skates, Rays
and Chimeras
of British Columbia

Also from the Royal BC Museum

Spirits of the Coast: Orcas in Science, Art and History
edited by Martha Black, Lorne Hammond and Gavin Hanke,
with Nikki Sanchez

Marine Mammals of British Columbia
by John K.B. Ford

Nature Guide to the Victoria Region
edited by Ann Nightingale and Claudia Copley

Carnivores of British Columbia
by David F. Hatler, David W. Nagorsen and Alison M. Beal

Royal BC Museum Handbook

SHARKS SKATES RAYS AND CHIMERAS
OF BRITISH COLUMBIA

GORDON MCFARLANE AND JACKIE KING

ROYAL **BC** MUSEUM

VICTORIA, CANADA

Sharks, Skates, Rays and Chimeras of British Columbia

Text copyright © 2020 by Gordon (Sandy) McFarlane and Jackie King

Published by the Royal BC Museum, 675 Belleville Street, Victoria, British Columbia, v8w 9w2, Canada.

The Royal BC Museum is located on the traditional territories of the Lekwungen (Songhees and Xwsepsum Nations). We extend our appreciation for the opportunity to live and learn on this territory.

Library and Archives Canada Cataloguing in Publication
Title: Sharks, skates, rays and chimeras of British Columbia /
    Gordon McFarlane and Jackie King.
Names: McFarlane, G. A., author. | King, J. R. (Jacquelynne R.), 1968- author.
    | Royal British Columbia Museum, issuing body.
Series: Royal British Columbia Museum handbook.
Description: Series statement: Royal BC Museum handbook
    | Includes bibliographical references and index.
Identifiers: Canadiana (print) 20200164503 | Canadiana (ebook) 20200164511
    | ISBN 9780772673350 (softcover) | ISBN 9780772673374 (EPUB)
    | ISBN 9780772673367 (Kindle) | ISBN 9780772673381 (PDF)
Subjects: LCSH: Sharks—British Columbia. | LCSH: Skates (Fishes)—British
    Columbia. | LCSH: Rays (Fishes)—British Columbia.
    | LCSH: Chimaeridae—British Columbia.
Classification: LCC QL638.6 .M34 2020 | DDC 597.309711—dc23

10 9 8 7 6 5 4 3 2 1

Printed and bound in Canada by Friesens.

100% FSC www.fsc.org MIX Paper from responsible sources FSC® C016245 Ancient Forest Friendly™ BIO GAS ENERGY PERMANENT

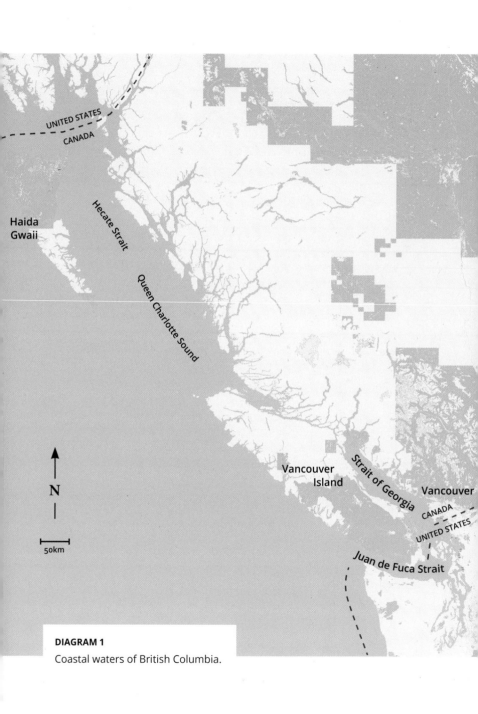

DIAGRAM 1

Coastal waters of British Columbia.

Contents

Foreword

Many new fishes, including new sharks and skates, have been discovered in BC waters since the publication of J.L. Hart's *Pacific Fishes of Canada* in 1973. Of the three chondrichthyan groups covered in the book you are now holding, sharks obviously receive the most attention from the public. I certainly was hooked following that classic film *Jaws*—my mother tried to cover my eyes during the gory scenes. Years later I pored over H. David Baldridge's book *Shark Attack* with ghoulish fascination, and I was probably the only child at my school who signed out all of the shark books from the library.

While the movie *Jaws* spawned public fascination, it also provoked a period of slaughter, with sharks paying a heavy toll for Peter Benchley's work of fiction. Fortunately, public perception has changed radically since the 1970s, in step with our increase in knowledge of marine life and recognition of ecosystem fragility. Now sharks, skates and rays almost have a cult following, and even chimeras are gaining recognition, as ghost sharks. We now see these fishes as essential parts of marine ecosystems. Aquatic tourists swim with sharks rather than seeing them shot on sight. Fear gave way to fascination.

Knowledge fuelled change, much the way it did since the 1960s for killer whales. Books like the one you now hold are the reason for much of today's changed perceptions. While sharks and their relatives have not yet reached the same status as marine mammals in the public eye, and sport fishing and commercial shark and skate fisheries still exist, we are now far more cognizant of harvest rates and other threats to marine life from our own behaviours, such as pollution and climate change.

While many will see sharks and stingrays only in public aquariums, and a fortunate few will go diving and experience cartilaginous fishes first-hand, and fewer still will keep sharks and stingrays in home aquariums, the vast majority of people will learn about chondrichthyans like I did: from books representing years of study and observation. This book by Gordon McFarlane and Jackie King is now, as Hart's book was in 1973, the new benchmark detailing diversity of chondrichthyan fishes in British Columbia, the deep history of our shark and skate fisheries, and the dark times for basking sharks, as well as the latest discoveries from recent exploration. Dive in.

— Gavin Hanke
  Curator of Vertebrate Zoology
  Royal BC Museum

Preface

Sharks! The very word conjures up images of dangerous, large, ferocious creatures with voracious appetites. This image couldn't be further from the truth for the vast majority of shark species—most species are cautious and placid, and many inhabit waters that exclude them from human contact. Much of the fear of sharks is driven by media reports or movies that sensationalize shark attacks despite their rarity. There is so much about sharks and their relatives that makes them fascinating, and we have a lot to learn.

Did you know that sharks inhabit the waters off British Columbia? Most people don't know that, and even more are surprised to discover that 15 species of sharks have been observed off British Columbia. As beguiling as sharks are, their flattened relatives, the skates and rays, which are found on the ocean floor and seem less threatening than sharks, are a group of fishes that people are also excited to discover and learn about. There are 17 species of skates and rays found in our waters. Probably the least known shark relative is the chimera—which, as the name implies, is a weird-looking fish that seems like a mash-up of several different species. There is one species of chimera in British Columbia, and although it is one of the most abundant fish that we have, few people know about it.

We wrote this book for everyone interested in learning more about sharks and their relatives in BC waters—the public, naturalists, students, researchers and anglers, as well as people who make their living on the water, such as commercial fishers and marine tourism workers. Although we used many references as sources of information, we avoided the traditional scientific writing style of in-text references to keep this book more readable; key references are listed under the bibliography. This book provides the most accurate and up-to-date information on sharks and their relatives in BC waters, and a substantial portion of the book is dedicated to species description and identification. The short descriptions of the biology and life history of the species presented in this book cannot do justice to this extraordinary group of animals. We hope that in addition to encouraging people to consider sharks and their relatives as valuable additions to our coastal fish community, worthy of respect, study, admiration and protection, this book will lead the reader to undertake more detailed study elsewhere.

We are both federal scientists who have conducted research and population assessments on sharks and skates. Fisheries and Oceans Canada provided us with the opportunity to write this book and with valuable data and information. We provide an overview of our personal research on methods for determining growth rates, age at maturity, and mortality rates; on our tagging and genetic studies for species distribution; on our feeding and ecosystem studies; and on our assessment and conservation work. As you can imagine, this work requires a team approach, both at sea, where we acquire the samples and data, and in the laboratory, where we analyze what we found. We are especially grateful to many colleagues at Fisheries and Oceans Canada, in the fishing industry, in non-governmental organizations and at university and government laboratories in the United States, Mexico and Japan who, over the years, worked with us directly in our stock assessment and research activities, or who saved samples or passed on observations from their own work: Schon Acheson, Bill Andrews, Brad Beaith, Richard Beamish, Ashleen Benson, Heather Brekke, Doug Brown, Scott Buchanan, Greg Cailliet, Steve Campana, Mark Cantwell, Ted Carter, Line Christensen, Ernie Cooper, Heidi Dewar, Nick Dulvy, Dave Ebert, Van Egan, Vince Gallucci, Sabrina Garcia, Chris Gburski, Graham Gillespie, Ken Goldman, Tom Helser, Vanessa Hodes, Craig Kastelle, Keith Ketchen, Suzanne Kohin, Karen Leask, James Logan, Tamee Mawani, Romney McPhie, Brian Mose, Chrys Neville, Oscar Sosa-Nishizaki, Tammy Norgard, Grady O'Neill, Dennis Rutherford, Takashi Sasaki, Mark Saunders, Ray Scarsbrook, Mahmood Shivji, Mike Smith, Paul Starr, Shawn Stebbins, Maria Surry, Ruston Sweeting, Mioko Taguchi, Ian Taylor, Bruce Turris, Nev Venables, Scott Wallace, Bernie White, Paul Winchell, Ruth Withler, Chris Wood, Malcolm Wyeth, Jennifer Yakimishyn, Lynne Yamanaka and Tyler Zubkowski. We thank the officers and crews of the Fisheries and Oceans Canada research vessels CCGS *G.B. Reed*, CCGS *W.E. Ricker* and CCGS *Neocaligus*, along with numerous charter vessels, for their support in conducting our field research. We also thank fishers throughout the Pacific Rim including Canada, the United States, Japan and Mexico, and the state and federal agencies of those nations that assisted the fishers in forwarding the tags with recovery and biological information.

We thank Gavin Hanke and again Maria Surry for their thorough reviews of an earlier draft of this book. We thank Jay Orr and Duane Stevenson for sharing their research on the taxonomy of north Pacific skates for inclusion in this book. In addition, all species illustrations are provided courtesy of Fisheries and Oceans Canada—these illustrations have been developed over the years for outreach. We thank the illustrators Jennifer Stone, Jesse Woodward and Uko Gorter. We are especially grateful to the publishing team: Eve Rickert, Jeff Werner, Eva van Emden, Grace Yaginuma, Lana Okerlund, Catherine Plear and Annie Mayse.

We also thank Andy Murch, who provided the underwater photographs. All proceeds of this book are going to Andy's Predators in Peril conservation project.

— Gordon (Sandy) McFarlane and Jackie King
  Pacific Biological Station
  Fisheries and Oceans Canada

IMAGE 1

Authors sampling bluntnose sixgill shark that washed up on shore of the Strait of Georgia near Comox, BC.

PHOTO: G. MCFARLANE / B. ANDREWS.

Biology

What are chondrichthyans?

Sharks, skates, rays and chimeras are chondrichthyans, a name derived from Greek *chondr*, meaning cartilage, and *ichthys*, meaning fish. As their name suggests, all these fishes have a simple internal skeleton composed of a light and flexible tissue called cartilage, which separates this group of fishes from all remaining jawed fishes, which have skeletons and other structures made of bone. The only bone-like materials in chondrichthyans are found in their teeth, in their scales in small amounts and sometimes in their vertebrae. Other distinguishing characteristics are paired nares (nostrils), a tough skin usually covered with small tooth-like scales called denticles, external claspers in males used in mating, and large oil-enriched livers. Since chondrichthyans lack the air-filled swim bladder found in the bony fishes to regulate buoyancy, they must swim continuously to avoid sinking, and they increase their buoyancy with low-density oils stored in their large livers. Some sharks and most skates and rays will rest on the sea floor, using their large mouths to pump water over their gills, while others move continuously to drive seawater through their mouths and over their gills to extract oxygen.

Taxonomy

All animals are descendants from small, simple animals that inhabited the world's oceans over 500 million years ago. During the next 100 million years, these simple animals evolved into recognizable fish-like ancestors often described as the jawless fishes. By the Late Silurian to Early Devonian periods (420 to 405 MYA), jawless fishes had reached their acme and began vanishing from the fossil record. The only jawless ancestors to survive today are the hagfishes and lampreys. By the time jawless fishes were in decline, the ancestors of all major groups of modern fishes had evolved, so that the Devonian period, with its diversity of fish species, is commonly known as the Age of Fishes. Sharks and their relatives—the skates, rays and chimeras—were much more common and diverse in the fossil record than they are now, with over 3,000 species. Today we know only about 1,100 living species, but this list is growing as new species are discovered.

Biologists use the characteristics of organisms to classify them into groups within a hierarchical system that goes from general to specific: kingdom (e.g., Animalia—all animals), phylum (e.g., Chordata—animals with backbones), class (e.g., Chondrichthyes—cartilaginous jawed fishes), order, family, genus and species. A species is assigned a single scientific two-part name made up of its genus and species designation. The scientific name is usually italicized, with the first letter of the genus capitalized and the species name written in lower case. There is no final, definitive set of hierarchical groups. Instead, the classification of organisms is continuously changing as we find new fossils and learn more about the evolution and biology of species living today. This certainly is true of the classification of fishes.

At the broadest level, fishes are classified into three main groups: the jawless fishes (Agnatha), which include hagfishes and lampreys; the cartilaginous fishes (Chondrichthyes), which include sharks, skates, rays and chimeras; and the bony fishes (Osteichthyes), which include all fishes with bony skeletons, including the somewhat shark-shaped ray-finned fishes such as paddlefishes and sturgeons. It is important to note that the living jawless fishes also have cartilaginous skeletons, so in that sense they are cartilaginous fishes, but because they do not have jaws, they are grouped separately from the sharks and their relatives.

The class Chondrichthyes contains two living subclasses: the Elasmobranchii (also called elasmobranchs), which are all sharks, skates and rays; and the Holocephali (also called holocephalans), which are all chimeras. Elasmobranchs are divided into nine orders. Eight of these are "typical" sharks, and the other order, the Rajiformes, contains all skates and rays. Sharks and their relatives today seem to be a fairly conservative group with an easily recognizable body, but deeper in the fossil record, there were some really bizarre sharks and chimeras that rival the best creations from science fiction.

Morphology

Sharks are one of the most easily recognized animals in the world. Most sharks are more or less fusiform (that is, football shaped) or cylindrical, although some—for example, angel sharks (Squatinidae)—have a more flattened body. Sharks have rigid dorsal fins and five to seven pairs of gill openings (see Diagram 2, page 48). Some sharks have dorsal fins with a bony spine along the leading edge. In all sharks, the gill openings are positioned just ahead of the pectoral fins. In sharks, the pectoral fins are not attached to the head, as they are for skates and rays. Most sharks have an anal fin. Sharks lack a swim bladder but have a large, oily liver to help them achieve neutral buoyancy. Sharks have numerous rows of teeth, which are replaced rapidly when necessary. Almost all sharks live in marine habitats, but some species are known to enter brackish estuaries and bays, and some species can be found entering rivers and lakes connected to the sea.

Skates and rays are easily distinguished from other fish by their flattened bodies, which allow them to live on or very close to the bottom of the ocean, where they bury themselves in mud or sand to ambush prey and avoid predators. However, a number of species, like the manta rays, have become nektonic (they swim well clear of the sea floor), using their enlarged pectoral fins to "fly" through the water. Some species of rays have unique adaptations such as specialized electric organs capable of producing a painful electric charge (electric rays) and modified scales—or barbs—capable of giving a piercing sting (stingrays).

The flattened bodies of skates have large, wing-like pectoral fins that are attached to the sides of the head and are continuous along the sides of the body (see Diagram 3, page 116). Together the head, body and wings form what is called a disc, although the overall shape of a skate is triangular or diamond shaped. The gill slits of a skate are on the underside (ventral surface) of the head. Skates have long tails, and those in British Columbia have two small dorsal fins near the tip of the tail. The caudal fin, or tail fin, is either very small or absent. The pelvic fins have two lobes, sometimes with a deep notch separating the lobes. Many skate species have numerous small prickles on the disc and tail, giving these areas a rough texture, and a row of thorns along the back and tail is also typical for many species. Mature male skates have rows of enlarged thorns near the eyes and wing tips, called malar and alar thorns, respectively. The alar thorns are very sharp. During copulation, they stimulate the female skate and anchor the male firmly against the female's body and pelvic fin.

Rays are similar to skates in their general shape, but they show some differences in their fin and tail structure, defensive spines and reproductive biology, which we discuss in "Reproductive biology" below. Rays have pelvic fins with only one lobe. The tail of a ray is more slender and whip-like than that of a skate, and there is usually a stinging spine midway along the length of the tail. Dorsal fins are usually absent, although a few species have a single dorsal fin near the base of the tail. Male rays lack malar or alar thorns.

Chimeras, also known as ratfish or ghost sharks, have soft, elongated bodies. They have a prominent, large head with a single gill opening, paddle-shaped pectoral fins and a long, pointed whip-like tail resembling the tail of a rat. Chimeras have a large venomous spine just ahead of the large first dorsal fin, and most have a long, low second dorsal fin that sometimes has an undulating profile, giving the appearance of two fins. Chimeras have an anal fin, which can be separate or joined to the caudal fin. The teeth of chimeras are fused into three pairs of tooth plates; the two frontmost pairs of teeth look similar to a rodent's, hence the common name ratfish or rabbitfish for some species. In fact, the genus name of the ratfish in our waters (*Hydrolagus*) means "water rabbit." Males have a prominent denticle-covered clasper on their head, thought to be used to hold the female during reproduction.

Reproductive biology

Chondrichthyans have fascinating modes of reproduction. Many species exhibit courtship behaviour where the male conveys his intentions with repeated biting of the female near the fins, abdomen or gill slits. Eventual success in courtship results in the male holding onto the female with a bite to get into position. Once in position, the male inserts its claspers into the female's reproductive tract to deliver the sperm packets. This internal fertilization occurs in all chondrichthyans.

The development of embryos occurs either externally (these species are called oviparous, or egg-laying) or internally (referred to as viviparous, or live-bearing, species). Oviparous, or egg-laying, chondrichthyans form a leathery egg case around the fertilized eggs and then deposit the egg cases on the bottom of the ocean. Most oviparous species in the northeast Pacific produce cases containing only a single egg; however, the big skate produces cases containing as many as eight eggs. The egg cases, which are sometimes called mermaid purses, have an overall appearance that is unique to the species, making it useful for identification. Egg cases vary in shape and colour, and commonly have horns or tendrils extending from the corners. These horns and tendrils help to anchor the egg case to the sea floor to provide some stability and safety for the developing embryo, which can take up to a year to mature. Embryos develop within the egg case, obtaining nourishment from yolk sacs, and emerge as miniature versions of the adults.

Viviparous, or live-bearing, chondrichthyans retain their embryos internally and eventually give birth to live young. The developing embryos may be nourished in one of two ways. In ovoviviparity, also known as aplacental viviparity, the embryos are nourished entirely from a large yolk sac. Once the yolk has been used, the embryo is fully developed and is born shortly thereafter. In a few species of sharks, aplacental viviparity can be taken to the extreme, with supplemental nourishment provided through intrauterine (within the uterus) cannibalism! This can take the form of oophagy (egg eating), when some of the developing embryos, once they have used up their yolk sacs, eat developing eggs. In the most extreme cases, the largest embryo will actually attack and eat smaller developing embryos in a process known as adelphophagy (literally "eating one's brother").

The other mode of internal nourishment is placental viviparity. In this mode, the nourishment of the yolk sac is used up early on in development, but the yolk sac also connects to the uterine wall, forming a simple placenta. The yolk-sac placenta transfers nutrients directly from the adult female to the embryo. Viviparous chondrichthyans have a long gestation period typically ranging from nine to twelve months. Notable exceptions are the Pacific spiny dogfish, with a gestation period of over two years, and basking sharks, which are thought to have a gestation period of over three years. In the northeast Pacific, depending on the species, litter sizes can range from one to more than a hundred young.

Role in the ecosystem

Sharks have the public image of voracious predators, and indeed many species are apex predators, feeding at the top of the food chain on bony fishes and marine mammals. There are a few exceptions to this, the most notable being the basking shark, which actually filter-feeds on plankton. Some shark species are small, such as the brown catshark, which limits its feeding to small bony fishes and invertebrates. And it should be noted that some sharks switch favourite prey items depending on the ecosystem and the time of the year, and with age. For example, Pacific spiny dogfish in the spring in the Strait of Georgia feed primarily on Pacific herring, while those inhabiting the southwest coast of Vancouver Island in summer feed primarily on krill.

Because many sharks are apex predators, they play an important role in maintaining marine ecosystems by controlling the populations of many prey species. Sharks, being highly mobile, also play an important role in transferring food energy within and across ecosystems over broad spatial and temporal scales. In addition, sharks provide food for other large marine predators.

Recent evidence has showed that killer whales are frequent predators of some shark species, such as Pacific sleeper sharks and great white sharks. California sea lions (*Zalophus californianus*) have been reported to feed on thresher and blue sharks, and Pacific spiny dogfish are prey to harbour seals and California and Steller sea lions. Catsharks as well as blue sharks and Pacific angel sharks are reported to be important in the diet of northern elephant seals. In some cases, smaller sharks are preyed upon by larger sharks—for example, bluntnose sixgill sharks are known to eat Pacific spiny dogfish.

In natural (undisturbed) ecosystems, sharks are generally abundant and diverse, and the depletion of sharks can cause dramatic ecological changes. Recent studies show that after the removal of large sharks in an area, mid-sized predators such as smaller sharks, skates and rays, as well as longer-lived marine species such as tunas, marine mammals and turtles, increased dramatically.

As you'd expect, an increase in these mid-sized predators has an immediate effect on their prey populations. For example, overfishing the largest predatory sharks along the Atlantic coast of the United States led to a population explosion within the ray, skate and small-shark prey species in this area. This had cascading effects through the ecosystem.

IMAGE 2
Baby bluntnose sixgill shark captured on a Fisheries and Oceans Canada Pacific spiny dogfish survey. PHOTO: V. HODES / M. SURRY.

The primary prey of these species, namely scallops, was depleted, followed by a population decline in their alternative prey species, such as clams and oysters. This decline in scallops, clams and oysters has caused economic hardships for those fisheries, an unforeseen consequence of overfishing the sharks at the top of the food chain.

Another example of the benefits of healthy shark populations is seen in Australia. The presence of sharks alters the behaviour of their prey, in this case dugongs and green sea turtles. When sharks are present, their prey are more cautious and reduce their grazing of eelgrass beds. As a result, local eelgrass beds do not become overgrazed, and organisms that live in those beds are more abundant, with a more robust ocean-floor ecosystem.

Skates, rays and chimeras are not apex predators but still fill an important role in marine food webs. The flattened bodies of skates and rays enable them to swim along the ocean bottom searching for prey. Their ideal food consists of molluscs, crabs, small fish and worms that inhabit the ocean floor, but they will also feed on carrion (decaying flesh), which helps to maintain the ocean floor's health. Skates and rays use vibrations in the sand and water to detect prey, and once they have found a meal, they flap their wings (pectoral fins), digging into the sand and displacing sand and organisms into the water column. The small organisms displaced by this process also provide a good food source for other species taking advantage of the excavation. Skates and rays are a food source for larger predators such as large bony fish, sharks and many marine mammals, thereby transferring energy to other levels in the food chain.

Chimeras feed primarily on invertebrates but also take the occasional small fish. Chimeras themselves are eaten by numerous bony fishes and sharks, including bluntnose sixgill sharks, tope sharks and Pacific spiny dogfish. In British Columbia, chimeras are extremely abundant and, as with the skates and rays, offer a source of energy to several levels in the food chain.

Although it is clear that chondrichthyans play a role in maintaining ecosystem health and diversity, there are very few directed studies investigating the specific roles of these species. Knowing the diet and biology of chondrichthyans continues to be an essential research requirement for their conservation and for understanding ecosystem function.

Conservation and Management in British Columbia

The most common species of elasmobranch (sharks, skates and rays) currently encountered in BC waters are Pacific spiny dogfish, big skate and longnose skate. Also commonly encountered are Pacific sleeper shark, salmon shark, bluntnose sixgill shark, brown catshark, blue shark, sandpaper skate and roughtail skate. Great white sharks are rare, as are shortfin mako and hammerhead sharks. There are only two verified occurrences of shortfin mako in BC waters, and what few records there are of hammerhead sharks are historical catches from the 1950s.

New species still appear in our waters, but these are not species new to science. Newly detected species "appear" because of the hit-and-miss nature of deep-sea sampling. In 2005, a single specimen of Pacific white skate along with specimens of fine-spined skate were captured by trawl off the west coast of Vancouver Island. The commander skate has been encountered only once within BC waters; it was captured in a research survey in 2009 within Queen Charlotte Sound. Our most recent addition to the list of species known to occur in this area, the Pacific angel shark, was spotted and photographed by a recreational scuba diver off Clover Point in Victoria, BC (southwest Vancouver Island), in 2016.

Conservation

Elasmobranchs tend to be unproductive—that is, they mature slowly and produce few offspring compared to other fishes, and therefore fishing must be maintained at a relatively low level if it is to be sustainable. In the past, these species have been a low priority for management agencies;

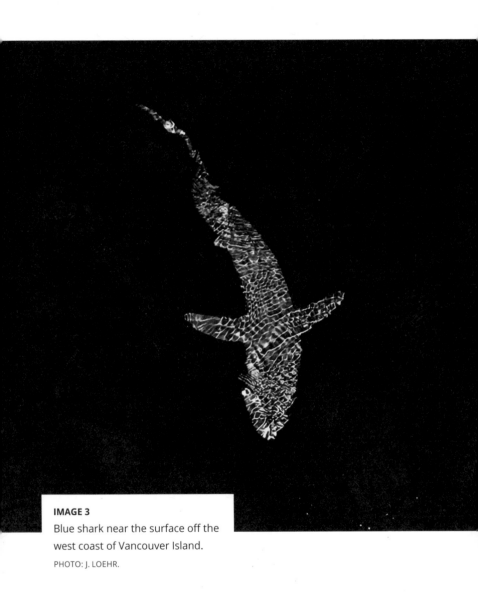

IMAGE 3

Blue shark near the surface off the west coast of Vancouver Island.

PHOTO: J. LOEHR.

however, over the last few decades, sharks and skates have received increasing attention as it has become even more apparent that many of these species are becoming severely depleted in many areas of the world.

Several international organizations have begun to promote conservation of some shark, skate and ray species. The Food and Agriculture Organization of the United Nations released the International Plan of Action for the Conservation and Management of Sharks in 1998 urging immediate action to better document and conserve shark and ray species. The Shark Specialist Group of the International Union for Conservation of Nature (IUCN) provides information and guidance to governments and non-governmental organizations associated with the conservation of threatened shark species and populations. Their Red List classifies species into nine groups, ranging from Least Concern to Extinct. The group released their report *Global Status of Oceanic Pelagic Sharks and Rays* in 2009.

As a final step of international protection, the Convention on International Trade in Endangered Species of Wild Fauna and Flora attempts to protect endangered species through international trade regulations, such as restrictions on import and export. The convention currently lists two shark species found in Canadian waters under "Appendix II": great white sharks and basking sharks. In May 2007 and again in March 2010, two other species were considered for listing under the appendix—the porbeagle shark (a type of mackerel shark found in Atlantic Canada) and the Pacific spiny dogfish—but ultimately were not listed.

Canada released its *National Plan of Action for the Conservation and Management of Sharks* in 2007, and in 2012 a progress report on the plan summarized the current status of shark-conservation efforts in Canada. The most intensive conservation assessment in Canada is conducted by the Committee on the Status of Endangered Wildlife in Canada (COSEWIC), which reviews the population status of potentially endangered wildlife and categorizes each population according to its relative abundance or health. These recommendations are then passed on to the Canadian government for possible action under the Species at Risk Act. If the population or species is listed under the Species at Risk Act, the federal government has a legal obligation to implement management and action plans, and in the instance of Endangered listings, to also assess the recovery potential.

Eleven Pacific coast elasmobranch species have been reviewed by COSEWIC in Canada to date; three of these species have been listed under Canada's Species at Risk Act. The basking shark was recently listed as Endangered, and the bluntnose sixgill and tope sharks were both listed as species of Special Concern. The other eight elasmobranch species assessed were not listed under the Species at Risk Act; they were classified by the committee as Data Deficient or Not at Risk. One was classified as Special Concern (the Pacific spiny dogfish), but its listing under the act is still being considered.

In recent years, efforts to publicize the vulnerability of sharks have led to the perception that there are no shark species that can withstand any form of fishing pressure, but this is not the case. Life-history traits vary greatly across shark species, and some species in British Columbia, including Pacific spiny dogfish, big skate and longnose skate, are capable of sustaining a fishery if the fishing levels are based on scientific advice. The perception that sharks cannot be sustainably fished has led many environmental groups and some government agencies to suggest complete bans on fishing, and this in turn has resulted in the unintended consequence of reduced support for the science that would be needed to formulate sustainable management plans for directed and incidental fisheries. A number of jurisdictions (notably in the United States, Australia and Canada) have successful shark management and conservation programs, which can serve as models for other countries.

Management

Canada supports the international programs mentioned above and the principles that underlie them for the conservation of sharks and other elasmobranchs. Canada's Oceans Act encourages "the wide application of the precautionary approach to the conservation, management and exploitation of marine resources in order to protect these resources and preserve the marine environment." The precautionary approach is an approach to policy making that recognizes that there is uncertainty about consequences and is therefore based on caution and sound risk management. Incorporating such an approach into management regimes for sharks is warranted because of their life history, which makes them particularly vulnerable to the long-term effects of overfishing. They mature late, grow relatively slowly and produce few offspring compared to bony fish, and this means that shark stocks can be depleted rapidly and they recover slowly. The other reason for adopting the precautionary approach is that limitations in scientific and stock-status information create uncertainty about policy consequences.

Developing a fishery-harvest strategy that incorporates the precautionary approach requires a number of activities. Information such as catch reports must be gathered and analyzed, resource users need to be consulted, and regulations must be evaluated and amended to conform with new requirements and information. Canada manages its fisheries through developing and carrying out integrated fisheries-management plans, research, consultation and fisheries monitoring.

These fisheries-management measures are applied relatively consistently throughout Canada; however, each region (that is, the Atlantic, Pacific and Arctic) has its own detailed development, application and enforcement. Fisheries and Oceans Canada develops integrated fisheries-management plans to identify the main objectives and requirements for a particular fishery (including directed shark and skate fisheries and fisheries that catch sharks and skates as bycatch) and the management measures to achieve these objectives. Fisheries-management plans communicate basic information about the fishery and its management, including licensing and quotas, to department staff, co-management boards and other stakeholders.

Fisheries and Oceans Canada does stock assessment and management for the Pacific spiny dogfish, big skate and longnose skate. The fisheries that capture these species are managed through area quotas. Other shark and skate species are caught and discarded as part of the commercial fishery; however, 100 per cent at-sea monitoring by observers or video monitoring means that almost all bycatch and discard totals are now recorded for all shark and skate species. This monitoring is used for trawl fisheries (both initiated in 1996), hook-and-line fisheries and trap fisheries (initiated in 2006). Other measures used in the management of sharks in the Pacific region include a ban on shark finning, new limits on recreational fishing and codes of conduct to reduce mortality from accidental capture.

Shark finning, the practice of removing the fins and discarding the remainder of the carcass while at sea, was banned in Canada in June 1994. The ban applies to Canadian waters and Canadian licensed vessels fishing outside of Canadian waters. To help enforce this ban, the number of fins sold must be in proportion to the number of carcasses landed (fin weight must be 5 per cent of dressed carcass weight), ensuring that accounts of total sharks harvested are accurate.

The rules for recreational fishing changed in 2010. Before that time, sharks fell into the "other species" category of recreational fishing, which allowed each harvester to retain up to 20 sharks a day. After federal consultations with the Sport Fishing Advisory Board, the daily limit for all sharks was changed to zero, with the exception of the salmon shark and Pacific spiny dogfish. The daily limit for salmon sharks was reduced to one with a possession limit of two, and the daily limit and possession limit for Pacific spiny dogfish were changed to four and eight, respectively. Skates are managed as a single category, with a daily limit of one, a possession limit of two and no annual limit.

Encounter protocols (a code of conduct) for a shark species make sure harvesters take every measure to avoid incidental capture of that species. As of the 2010 commercial fishing season, encounter protocols were implemented for the Pacific basking shark, which is listed as Endangered under the Species at Risk Act. The protocol specifies that fishing gear cannot be set or hauled when the shark is 10 metres from the vessel or visible from the water's surface, and any incidentally caught shark must be released in a way that causes the least harm.

In 2013, Fisheries and Oceans Canada developed a code of conduct for shark encounters in commercial, aquaculture and recreational fisheries to reduce bycatch and entanglement deaths of the bluntnose sixgill shark, tope shark and other Canadian Pacific shark species. (This code does not cover the basking shark, which has its own code of conduct, developed in 2010.) The handling guidelines in the code of conduct may be useful for fishers who wish to release salmon sharks and Pacific spiny dogfish, but the code of conduct does not apply to the directed fisheries for those species.

Fisheries

Global catch statistics

Over the last few decades, with the decline of many traditional finfish stocks, there has been a growing interest in commercial fishing of elasmobranch fisheries targeting species from wide-ranging pelagic (free-swimming) sharks to demersal (bottom-dwelling), deepwater skates. Overall, global commercial landings (that is, fish harvested and brought to land) of elasmobranchs reported to the Food and Agriculture Organization of the United Nations have risen steadily from approximately 200,000 tonnes in the 1940s to over 800,000 tonnes by the late 1990s, peaking at about 888,000 tonnes in 2000. This increase reflects rapidly emerging markets for their meat and valuable fins. Between 2000 and 2012, recorded landings declined to about 750,000. These declines were initially assumed to be the result of better management by some nations, such as the introduction of quotas or increased bycatch monitoring; however, recent analysis indicates that the decline in reported landings is the result of declining populations. It is also now accepted that reported landings are a gross underestimation of true catches.

In addition to directed fishing, many species have high mortality as bycatch in fisheries targeting more productive bony fishes. This mortality is unsustainable and generally unrestricted or difficult to restrict. Recent estimates of total catches, including bycatch and discards, indicate that global catch levels probably reached between 1.4 and 1.7 million tonnes annually, which is about twice the reported catch.

Over the last decade, these alarming numbers have made conservation groups and management agencies aware of the need to assess and manage the world's elasmobranch populations. Unfortunately, after years of exploitation, many stocks are now considered fully exploited, declining or maintained at low levels. The immediate challenge for fisheries scientists is to obtain the basic life-history information needed to accurately assess elasmobranch stocks. This requires adapting traditional stock-assessment methods for the special needs of elasmobranch species, which are vulnerable to over-exploitation because of their low reproductive rates.

BC fisheries

Most people are unaware that there are shark and skate fisheries off our coast. Sharks and skates have been commercially exploited to varying degrees throughout BC waters since the mid- to late 1800s. Historically, fisheries were directed at Pacific spiny dogfish, bluntnose sixgill shark, tope shark, basking shark and white-spotted ratfish, and to a lesser extent some skate species, recorded only as generic "skate." In the late 1800s and early 1900s, Pacific spiny dogfish body and liver oil was sought after as a lubricant and as fuel for lighting and heating. During the late 1930s and 1940s, a large liver fishery occurred for Pacific spiny dogfish, bluntnose sixgill shark, tope shark, basking shark and white-spotted ratfish as a source of vitamin A, when World War II eliminated the traditional supplies of North Atlantic cod-liver oil. In their heyday, these fisheries averaged over 18,000 tonnes, and peaked in 1944 at approximately 32,000 tonnes. The majority of this catch was Pacific spiny dogfish. By the late 1940s, shark catches began to decline, and in 1947 vitamin A was first synthesized in the laboratory, removing the need for shark livers. By 1950 the demand for shark livers, and the directed fishery, effectively ended.

In the late 1950s and 1960s, perhaps the most disturbing shark fisheries took place: fishing to eradicate the Pacific spiny dogfish and basking shark. These species were vilified by fishers as voracious predators of other commercially important fish. The Canadian government conducted a number of eradication programs that encouraged fishers to kill Pacific spiny dogfish in exchange for cash payments, herring licences and increased herring quota.

These programs were not successful in eradicating Pacific spiny dogfish, even though they removed more than 2,000 tonnes a year. Unfortunately, similar programs did succeed in almost eradicating basking sharks off the BC coast. From 1955 to 1969, basking sharks were killed by a large blade mounted on the bow of a fisheries patrol vessel, the *Comox Post*. Before the blade method of eradication, patrol vessels also tried shooting and harpooning, and at the time of the blade method, other patrol vessels were directed to opportunistically ram basking sharks. Also during this time, there was enough interest in the sport of harpooning basking sharks that the Canadian Pacific Railway promoted fishing for BC basking sharks in publicity releases. In total it has been estimated that somewhere between 1,000 and 2,600 basking sharks were killed between 1945 and 1970. Since the eradication program, basking sharks are rarely seen in BC waters.

Since the early 1970s, elasmobranch catches off the coast of British Columbia have been increasing, mirroring the increasing catches worldwide. In the 1970s and 1980s, catches (landed and discarded) of elasmobranchs in British Columbia (excluding the Pacific spiny dogfish) averaged 550 tonnes a year. Catches increased to an average of 1,350 tonnes in the late 1990s and peaked at 2,700 tonnes in 2000 (as a result of directed fisheries for big skate and longnose skate). In recent years (2013 to 2017) the average catch (excluding the Pacific spiny dogfish) has declined to approximately 1,500 tonnes. Of the 32 species of elasmobranchs in (or thought to be in) BC waters, targeted fisheries currently exist for only three species: Pacific spiny dogfish, big skate and longnose skate.

By 1977, a food fishery for Pacific spiny dogfish was firmly established in BC waters, using trawl fishing concentrated mainly in the Strait of Georgia. Production peaked in 1979 at 4,334 tonnes, but by 1980 the supply of fish seemed to be declining, and fishing shifted to grounds off the west coast of Vancouver Island. Even with the decline in catch in the Strait of Georgia, total catches (landed and discarded) in BC waters during the 1980s, 1990s and early 2000s remained relatively high, ranging from 5,000 to 7,000 tonnes per year, with the majority of these fish coming from the west coast of Vancouver Island. In 2006 a new management system was implemented for all groundfish fisheries, including sharks and skates. As a consequence, targeting of Pacific spiny dogfish declined dramatically throughout British Columbia, and coastwide catches declined to less than 1,000 tonnes.

The first recorded landings of skate in British Columbia occurred in 1911; however, landings throughout most of the 1900s were low, ranging from 20 to 470 tonnes annually. As skates were not a targeted fishery during this time period, it is assumed that most of the catch was discarded at sea. New market opportunities for skate developed in the mid-1990s, and a directed fishery for big skate and longnose skate began, mostly in Hecate Strait and Queen Charlotte Sound, with annual landings averaging about 1,500 tonnes from 1996 to 2002, when trip landing limits were implemented. Catches declined steadily, and in 2013, quotas and management areas were established for these two species, with quotas of approximately 1,000 tonnes for big skate and 450 tonnes for longnose skate across fishing sectors and areas. Catches have remained low, well below the quotas, mainly owing to a decreasing market price for skate and rising fishing costs.

Shark species incidentally encountered in BC fisheries include blue shark, salmon shark, tope shark, bluntnose sixgill shark, Pacific sleeper shark, common thresher shark and brown catshark. Since 1996, total BC incidental catches (landings and discards) of all shark species, excluding Pacific spiny dogfish (with a catch declining from 3,000 to 1,000 tonnes annually), is typically less than 100 tonnes per year. For skate, average annual discards are approximately 220 tonnes for big skate and 130 tonnes for longnose skate. Incidental catch of all other skate species (landings and discards) is approximately 50 tonnes per year.

Sharks are incidentally encountered in recreational fisheries in BC waters, but directed effort is likely low. In 2010, given general conservation concerns about sharks, Fisheries and Oceans Canada implemented a no-recreational-fishing policy for sharks with a requirement for the release of any incidental catches. There are two exceptions to this: one is for Pacific spiny dogfish (with a daily limit of four), since commercial fishery quotas exist; the other is for salmon shark (daily limit of one). Recreational fishers argued that since salmon sharks are targeted by recreational fishers in Alaska, and since they are common in BC waters, access to this resource should be available.

Information on recreational catches of sharks is available only categorized into Pacific spiny dogfish and a combined shark category. The Pacific spiny dogfish recreational catch data for 2012 to 2016 indicates that the majority that are encountered are released (23,000 to 66,000 fish per year) and only 3,000 to 6,000 fish per year retained. Approximately 4,000 to 27,000 other sharks are released per year, and anecdotal information indicates that these are mainly salmon sharks and blue sharks. Since salmon sharks are the only other species that can be retained in the recreational fishery, the estimated 500 to 2,000 retained fish per year are most likely salmon sharks, but it cannot be verified that other shark species are not also retained. Additionally, although recreational fishing for skates is permitted, the recreational catches are not well documented.

The more recent declines of both directed and incidental catches for all elasmobranch species are not attributed solely to declines in abundance but also reflect Canadian efforts for sustainable management coupled with conservation policy.

Difficulty in assessing stock status

The general consensus among fisheries scientists today is that traditional population models for bony fishes are less applicable to elasmobranchs because of their biological traits, such as extreme longevity, slow growth, late maturity, long gestation period and low reproductive potential (fecundity). As such, models that incorporate up-to-date biological information such as age, growth, mortality and fecundity have been used to assess elasmobranch populations in recent years, with varied levels of success. The accuracy of each population model depends on how well it can capture the dynamics of the natural world, including factors such as how a population of sharks will respond to changes in their habitat or prey abundance. A lot of population models require estimates of the demographics of the population, but with many species of elasmobranch, it is not possible to determine the age of a specimen. New ways of assessing elasmobranch populations are being developed that do not rely on firm age estimates, but include a range of estimates that can provide risk-based information. In addition, research on the biological traits of BC elasmobranchs can help biologists to develop the complex population models needed to estimate population responses to fishing and ecological changes.

IMAGE 4
Satellite tagging a blue shark off the west coast of Vancouver Island as part of a study to determine their movement patterns. PHOTO: J. KING / G. MCFARLANE.

Research in British Columbia

How do we study elasmobranchs?

It is now recognized that elasmobranchs play an integral role in marine ecosystems. In many, but not all, cases they are apex predators, meaning that they are at the top of the food chain. Despite the recognition of their important role in an ecosystem, as a group elasmobranchs remain some of the most under-studied marine fishes. Part of this lack of focus has been due to the historical cultural perspective of sharks and their relatives, namely that they are to be feared and have little economic value. Shifting societal perspectives have provided opportunities to expand necessary research on basic elasmobranch biology such as age determination, species distribution and feeding ecology, as well as conservation and sustainable use. In British Columbia, over the last three decades or so, research on elasmobranchs has contributed to filling the knowledge gaps in the areas of age determination, species distribution and feeding ecology for a number of species.

Age determination

Age information forms the foundation for calculations of growth and mortality rates, age at maturity, and longevity, ranking it among the most valuable of biological variables when attempting to assess species' susceptibility to exploitation. In bony fishes, researchers count annual bands in bony (calcified) structures such as fin rays, ear bones (called otoliths) or even scales. Aging a fish is much the same as counting tree rings. But the structures usually used to determine age in bony fishes are lacking in elasmobranchs. Instead, vertebral centra are most commonly used to determine age, as they are sufficiently calcified in many species. The next most commonly used structures are fin spines and caudal thorns. Even the ever-growing teeth of the white-spotted ratfish have been used to estimate age.

We ourselves have used thin sections of vertebral centra of big skate and longnose skate to determine their age. The vertebrae are removed from specimens, cleaned and air-dried. The individual centra are sectioned lengthwise to produce very thin slices. Under a microscope, annual bands created by seasonal calcium deposits are visible. In summer, when the fish grows rapidly, less dense calcium deposits are formed and appear as white bands in the centra. In winter, growth is slower, and the calcium deposits are denser and appear as a dark band. A light and dark band together typically marks one year of growth. Although there are less calcium deposits in chondrichthyans than in bony fishes, some techniques involving staining can enhance the small amount of calcium that exists.

However, some of the deepwater sharks, such as bluntnose sixgill sharks, do not have enough calcification in their vertebral centra to provide adequate growth information, even with common staining enhancement. The reasons might be related to their habitat, as these species inhabit dark, cold, deep water that may be low in calcium, or to the fact that they are from relatively primitive families. Our research in British Columbia on bluntnose sixgill sharks has identified that the neural arch—the inverted Y-shaped structure that straddles the spinal cord—can be used as alternate structures for age estimates.

The Pacific spiny dogfish possesses a prominent first dorsal spine, and seasonal differences in the enamel deposits on the outside of this spine have been used to provide age estimates. We and earlier Fisheries and Oceans Canada researchers have conducted much research on age determination of the Pacific spiny dogfish in British Columbia. One of the obstacles to simply counting annual bands on their spines has been that as the shark ages, the front of the spine tip wears away so that there is a lack of annual bands to count. We have been able to illustrate that the spine width where this wearing begins can be used to estimate the number of annual bands that are missing.

A difficult component of age-determination research is verifying the age-determination method. You must make sure that the metrics being used are realistic and that the results agree with estimates obtained through size-frequency analysis, back calculations or similar methods. The periodicity of band deposits must be determined to validate this aging method. For example, are the light and dark bands truly formed annually, or do they represent a shorter or longer time period? Sometimes as a fish grows, there can be major life or environmental events that change feeding behaviour or growth, and these events can result in false growth bands in the aging structure. These patterns, called checks, may be faint, incomplete or non-parallel to other bands. It is important that each age-determination method for each species is verified to make sure that the patterns counted for each species are indeed annual, and do not include checks.

The most accurate validation is through the use of direct measures of absolute age, such as the release of marked fish of known age. This type of research is rarely accomplished, however, since a vast number of chemically marked and tagged fish must be released to make sure enough fish are recaptured. Working with co-researchers from Fisheries and Oceans Canada, we conducted the largest shark-tagging and age-validation study for Pacific spiny dogfish. Over 17,800 of these sharks were captured, injected with an antibiotic called oxytetracycline, tagged and released. When injected into fish, oxytetracycline chemically marks skeletal structures by forming a distinct band that is visible under ultraviolet light. Tagged Pacific spiny dogfish were recovered through commercial and sport fisheries. Since the number of years between the tagging and subsequent recapture of the shark was known, we could count the number of bands deposited after the oxytetracycline mark and compare the total bands to the number of years that had passed to verify how many annual bands we were counting.

Another validation method is by using relative radiocarbon (known as carbon-14) in annual bands. In the late 1950s, atmospheric testing of atomic bombs led to an immediate increase in radiocarbon in the atmosphere. Over the next number of years this radiocarbon was absorbed by the oceans and was eventually incorporated by marine life into structures such as the exoskeletons of coral, the shells of bivalves,

IMAGE 5
Fisheries and Oceans Canada biologist releasing a big skate after sampling during a survey. PHOTO: L. GARDNER.

the bones of fish, and the cartilage of elasmobranchs. The dramatic increase from low radiocarbon levels in the late 1950s to high levels in the early 1970s creates a known time mark. Our collaborative research with researchers at Fisheries and Oceans Canada in the Atlantic region and US federal researchers has used this known time mark and radiocarbon levels to validate the age-determination method for longnose skate, using the vertebral centra, and for Pacific spiny dogfish, using the fin spines.

Species distribution

Sharks are very mobile fish, some moving many thousands of kilometres in the course of their seasonal patterns of feeding, mating and egg laying or pupping. Some species have different feeding grounds in winter and summer or specific areas that they use as nursery grounds for mating and pupping. In many cases, chondrichthyans segregate by size or sex, perhaps to avoid cannibalism on juveniles and small adults by larger adults. In addition, juveniles and smaller individuals eat smaller prey, which is generally found in different habitats from the larger prey of adults.

Why do scientists care about where a species can be found? It's important for scientists to understand species distribution and where different segments of each population live throughout the year so that they can assess population status, look at the impact of environmental changes and provide advice on conservation and fisheries management, such as setting suitable boundaries for management areas. Knowledge of special habitats, such as areas where skates deposit their egg cases, can help to protect certain life stages. Scientists develop tagging studies, use genetic information and analyze catch data from fisheries and research surveys to help determine a species' distribution. Some of British Columbia's sharks and rays are known from too few specimens for us to make any meaningful statements about overall distribution and seasonal movements.

Marking marine animals with tags is a research method that provides a variety of information. It is used to measure the size of a local population, what its mortality rate is and how successful stocking efforts are. It can also be used to measure the movements of individuals to understand daily behaviour and seasonal migration rates and routes. As discussed earlier, marking animals is part of measuring the age of individuals and validating growth-measurement methods.

Two common tagging methods are used to monitor fish populations. Movement mapping or tracking uses technologies like satellite tags or acoustic tags to tag fish and map their movements. Mark and recapture is a process where a small group of a particular fish species is captured, marked or tagged, and then released. The tag allows researchers to identify individual fish when recaptured and determine how far individual fish travelled and how long it took.

In British Columbia, we and US government researchers have employed satellite archival tags for tracking, and external tags for mark-and-recapture studies. The satellite archival tags are a fairly new technology that records temperature, depth and geographic location. The data are stored in the tag, and the tag relays information to a satellite, which in turn transmits data to the researcher.

We deployed these tags on blue sharks off the west coast of Vancouver Island in the summertime to investigate seasonal migration patterns. The data indicated that blue sharks moved southward over the course of the summer, down the coast of Washington, Oregon, California and Mexico. By late fall and early winter, one of the tagged sharks had moved offshore heading westward toward the central north Pacific.

We have also deployed satellite tags to study bluntnose sixgill sharks in the southern Strait of Georgia to investigate residency time and depth distribution. The bluntnose sixgill shark is a deepwater shark, but some sub-adults occupy the Strait of Georgia presumably until they mature, when they move offshore to deep water. Through tagging data, we now know that sub-adult bluntnose sixgill sharks in the Strait of Georgia show distinct seasonal movements, occupying shallower depths during the summer and even making forays into upper, warm surface waters. Those sub-adults appear to retreat to greater depths in winter.

We have conducted mark-and-recapture studies in British Columbia for Pacific spiny dogfish and big skate. The Pacific spiny dogfish study was the largest tagging study of a shark conducted in the world, with over 71,000 individuals captured, marked with an external tag and released back for subsequent recapture by the fisheries. Initial studies using the typical external tags deployed on bony fishes had a high rate of tag loss on the dogfish. In response, we developed an innovative tag that used specially designed titanium pins to anchor a disc to the dorsal fin. This new type of tag was so successful that tagged dogfish recaptured 20 years later still had the tag attached.

The study found that there was considerable variation in fish movement off the west coast of British Columbia. Pacific spiny dogfish tagged in the Strait of Georgia moved the least during the study, while those tagged off the west coast of Vancouver Island or in northern BC waters moved much farther. Pacific spiny dogfish from British Columbia were recaptured off the west coast of the United States and Alaska. Most impressive are the recaptures off the coast of Japan; most of these dogfish originated off the west coast of Vancouver Island or from northern British Columbia.

Mark and recapture was also used to study big skates in the northern area of Hecate Strait and in Queen Charlotte Sound. Like other fisheries, the big skate fishery showed seasonal patterns in fish presence and abundance, with the highest catches in north Hecate Strait in winter and in Queen Charlotte Sound in summer. Fisheries managers wanted to know if this reflected a seasonal migration of one single big skate population. Our tagging study indicated that this was not the case. In fact, the majority of tagged big skates were recaptured within 21 kilometres of their release location. The recapture was not dependent on season, telling scientists that the seasonality in the fishery catches was due to fishing-fleet behaviour and not seasonal migration of big skates. However, as with Pacific spiny dogfish, there were a few remarkable recaptures—some of the big skates from British Columbia had moved northward and were recaptured in the Gulf of Alaska and Bering Sea, the longest distance travelled being 2,340 kilometres.

Genetic studies can determine whether individuals captured in different regions are from the same or different populations. Along with colleagues in Fisheries and Oceans Canada and Japanese government researchers, we have conducted genetic studies to determine population structure for blue sharks captured in British Columbia and throughout the north Pacific to Japan. Analyses indicate that blue sharks in the north Pacific are indeed one single population, confirming the information from the satellite tag data that they are a highly migratory species. A similar study for salmon sharks that we conducted with Fisheries and Oceans Canada colleagues, Japanese government researchers and US federal and university researchers indicated that a single north Pacific population moves seasonally between the Gulf of Alaska in late summer and southern California waters.

One of the richest sources of information on species distribution and abundance is the fisheries that encounter chondrichthyans as catch or bycatch. Fishers fill in logbooks that often include species identification, location (often with latitude and longitude) and date of capture. In

British Columbia, it is mandatory to complete and submit logbooks, but in many cases species identification is missing or erroneous.

Within British Columbia, a unique program of catch monitoring has been in effect for over 20 years for the groundfish fleet. In addition to the requirement for fishers to complete logbooks, catch monitoring is done on all vessels, either by an independent at-sea observer or by electronic and video means. At-sea observers identify species caught and record the date, time, position (latitude and longitude) and depth, as well as the amounts of each species retained or released at sea. Electronic and video monitoring allows the independent verification of logbook information on trips without at-sea observers. These high-quality data have provided invaluable information about the distribution of BC chondrichthyans and have allowed researchers to map areas of high or low encounters for various species, particularly sharks. However, distributional data for some skates remains problematic owing to incomplete or incorrect identifications.

Feeding studies

There are few elasmobranch feeding studies, mainly because elasmobranchs are not highly abundant and analysis of stomach contents by stomach pumping or stomach removal is harmful or fatal. Information about a species' diet often comes from opportunistic sampling, information about bait depredation on longline gear, or applying the results of studies done in one region to another region. Understanding the movement patterns of sharks and skates helps scientists to understand their feeding behaviour. In particular, many sharks have developed a tight-knit relationship with their prey of choice so that they are highly migratory, following schools of prey moving around the north Pacific or moving to highly productive feeding areas. Feeding studies—particularly to answer questions about food webs, bioaccumulation of pollutants, and ecosystem function—are an important component to elasmobranch research, and will need to be a focus for future studies.

Information on diet has allowed scientists to identify the unique and important roles that elasmobranchs have in the ocean ecosystems. For example, scientists consider sharks to be keystone species, meaning that their removal will cause the whole food web to reorganize. In some cases, removing an apex predator from a food web causes other species to go extinct. It can even result in the complete collapse of the ecosystem structure. A number of scientific studies illustrate that depletions of shark populations have resulted in the loss of commercially important fish, such as tuna or shellfish species, or the loss of healthy coral reefs. Sharks keep many prey species from becoming too numerous and damaging their environment. Sharks feed on the sick and weak members of a population, and sometimes even scavenge dead carcasses. By doing so, they prevent the spread of disease, and by culling weaker animals, they also strengthen their prey species' gene pools.

Citizen science

As the public becomes more aware of the threats that sharks face from fishing, environmental damage and other factors, many want to help out by providing information on sightings during fishing or scuba diving to scientists and fisheries managers. There has been much debate on whether the data collected by citizen scientists is as useful as that collected by more traditional scientific methods, and in the past the scientific community has been reluctant to incorporate this information into their studies. However, as members of the public acquire training from government, university or conservation organizations on some basic principles of scientific observation and data gathering, citizen science is providing data that is both valuable and cost-effective. Just knowing "who, where and when" helps scientists to fill important information gaps about the shark species in British Columbia.

For example, in British Columbia the Shark Sightings Network was implemented by the federal government in 2007 to keep track of the endangered basking shark in our waters. Reports on basking sharks through the network help scientists track the recovery of this species in our region. The program has since expanded to include all shark species that the general public might observe at sea or washed ashore. A citizen scientist reported the first documented photographic record of the Pacific angel shark in BC waters. Without his efforts and cooperation, the presence of this shark may have gone undetected for many more years (as it has probably been in BC waters for years simply without having been seen or caught). Carcasses that wash ashore can provide scientists with valuable specimens for study, providing information on age, feeding biology, parasites, reproductive status and contaminant accumulation. Information on juvenile sharks can help scientists determine where nursery grounds for the species might be.

You can become involved as a citizen scientist for sharks by documenting and reporting captures and sightings of sharks, especially basking sharks, but with the exception of the Pacific spiny dogfish, in waters off British Columbia. You should document as many details of the encounter as possible, including the following:

- Photographs or video of the shark. Try to photograph the whole shark from its side including the dorsal fin, and if possible, take extra photos of the details, such as the underside of the head, the teeth, etc.
- The date and time of the encounter.
- The location. Be as specific as possible—for example, by including GPS data.
- Estimates of the total length and sex (males have claspers) of the shark.
- Any distinguishing features, such as the colour, visible scars, behaviours, visible wounds and swimming ability of the shark when observed or after release.
- Your name and contact information.

For more information, please see the Fisheries and Oceans Canada's "Report a Sighting or Incident" web page at www.pac.dfo-mpo.gc.ca /SharkSightings. The codes of conduct for shark encounters and basking shark encounters are also available on the website. You can report the information above through the website, to any fishery officer or through email at sharks@dfo-mpo.gc.ca.

From Feared and Loathed to Loved

Changing attitudes to sharks and their relatives—from destruction to conservation

Of all the chondrichthyans, sharks have suffered the most at our hands because of nothing more than ignorance and fear. (Although that's not to say that no one fears skates—skates resemble stingrays, some of which can have lethal stings.) There are records of shark attacks in the Mediterranean Sea as early as fifth century BCE, when the Greek writer Herodotus described shark attacks on shipwrecked sailors. Pliny the Elder, a Roman writer in the first century CE, wrote about small sharks biting skin divers.

Shark attacks are not common but have occurred throughout history, thereby fuelling societal fear. Shipwrecks and airplane crashes in Pacific waters during both world wars created widely reported shark-human interactions in offshore shark-infested waters. The infamous sinking of the USS *Indianapolis* and the subsequent shark attacks are the stuff of literary and movie legend. Since then, an increasing human population and increasing recreational use of coastal marine waters have resulted in relatively rare but well-publicized attacks. These real-life experiences have elevated our modern-day fear of sharks. To add insult to injury, fictional stories, such as *Jaws*, *The Shallows*, *47 Meters Down*, *Deep Blue Sea* or more slapstick offerings such as *Sharknado* and *3-Headed Shark Attack*, sensationalized the fear of sharks and brought the "experience" of a shark attack to our own living rooms.

This fear of sharks is exaggerated. The number of attacks per year is between 75 and 100 worldwide, of which between 5 and 10 result in fatalities. Compare this to the many tens of millions of times that people use the sea for work or recreation. It is surprising that the number of shark attacks is so low. In the United States, even considering only people who go to beaches, a person's chance of getting attacked by a shark is one in 11.5 million, and a person's chance of getting killed by a shark is less than one in 264.1 million. Most attacks happen to people in coastal areas surfing, skin or scuba diving or swimming.

Only a few species of shark are dangerous to humans. Out of more than 500 shark species, only a handful have been known to attack humans. Off the west coast of the United States (California to Washington State), almost all attacks are thought to be by great white sharks, with a few off California attributed to the shortfin mako shark and blue shark, and even one to the broadnose sevengill shark. Off Oregon and Washington, there have been a total of 17 shark attacks since 1974, none of which were fatal. All of these attacks were on surfers, and the attackers were confirmed to be great white sharks. To date there has never been a confirmed shark attack off British Columbia.

Along with this irrational fear, many sharks are loathed by commercial and recreational fishers because entangled sharks can do great damage to fishing gear and may also steal bait or fish catches. Sharks are also often blamed for causing declines in commercially important fishes by preying on them or even competing with them for food. Sharks in British Columbia have not been exempt. In the 1940s through the 1960s, the basking shark was blamed for the destruction of gillnets in the salmon fisheries and the loss of captured salmon. Similarly, Pacific spiny dogfish were considered a serious nuisance and blamed for the decline in abundance of valuable commercial and recreational fish through predation and blamed for destruction of fishing gear. These attitudes resulted in eradication programs for both species until the early 1970s, with the culling of hundreds of basking sharks and thousands of tonnes of Pacific spiny dogfish.

Fear and loathing of sharks in British Columbia is evident in historic newspaper headlines. Basking sharks attracted their share of coverage with descriptions like *menace* and *pests* in a series of articles including "Big Man-Eating Shark Caught Off Galiano" in the *Vancouver Sun* (September 23, 1947); "War Declared on B.C. Sharks" in the *Province* (February 3, 1943); "Removal of Shark Menace to Salmon Fishing Is Urged" in the *West Coast Advocate* (August 2, 1945); "Shark Hunters

Clean Up on West Coast Pests" in the *Province* (May 4, 1957); "Shark Panics Swimmers: Children Dash to Shore" in the *Colonist* (June 19, 1959); and "Ship Fights Sharks off B.C. Coast" in the *Vancouver Sun* (June 23, 1955).

Dogfish sharks were similarly described as *pests* and *villains* in articles like "Bounty on Dogfish Proposed to Abolish Great Pest" in the *Christian Science Monitor* (May 21, 1909) and "Dogfish—Puget Sound Villain" in the *Seattle Times* magazine (August 17, 1958).

Not all societies have hated sharks; on the contrary, some have revered them. In British Columbia the Pacific spiny dogfish was adopted as a totemic animal by some clans of First Nations. In many Pacific Island societies, shark worship was common: it was believed that sharks had supernatural powers and could provide protection.

In recent years, society has come to realize that sharks play an important role in ecosystems, and that they are vulnerable to extinction. Shark-conservation efforts are on the rise, with major international organizations publicizing issues such as illegal shark harvesting, trade or finning, and providing scientific evidence of declining abundance of many species. The need to manage shark fisheries sustainably is a priority for many regional fisheries organizations and government agencies. In Canada, a national plan of action produced by the federal government prioritizes sustainable fisheries management for the conservation of sharks. However, although the public is now beginning to see sharks as iconic and worthy of respect, that is not to say that the battle is won; a recent Australian study suggests that for each media report on the importance of shark conservation, there are five reports sensationalizing shark attacks.

Ecotourism

Perhaps in the future, sharks will be worth more alive than dead. Economically, the value of global shark fisheries has been estimated conservatively at close to US$1 billion annually, although this does not include the value of shark products consumed domestically in many countries. These fisheries (both directed and bycatch) continue to be an

IMAGE 6

Processing Pacific spiny dogfish for the food fish market during the modern fishery era.

PHOTO: FISHERIES AND OCEANS CANADA.

important source of income to fishers in many countries. On the other hand, ecotourism in the form of shark diving has become a burgeoning industry generating millions of dollars for local economies worldwide. In one recent study, it was estimated that the global shark-tourism industry (defined as observing sharks from boats, snorkelling or scuba diving) involves nearly 600,000 watchers or divers, supports about 10,000 jobs and is valued at around US$314 million annually, not including the associated revenues from travel, food and accommodation. One economic projection suggested that the landed value of global shark fisheries will be surpassed by the value of ecotourism over the next 15 to 20 years.

In British Columbia, shark tourism began in the mid- to late 1970s, when bluntnose sixgill sharks were seen in relatively shallow waters off Hornby Island in the Strait of Georgia and in Barkley Sound off the west coast of Vancouver Island. Throughout the 1980s and 1990s, these areas became destination dives for recreational scuba divers. Since this time a decrease in sightings (although not necessarily a decrease in the number of sharks), attributed mainly to environmental changes such as increased water temperatures that limit the sharks to deeper waters, have led to a decrease in the number of scuba tourists in these areas.

Challenges for the Future

Over the last 400 million years, sharks and their relatives have proven themselves to be one of the most, if not *the* most, resilient and adaptable animals in the world's oceans. This all changed in the last century when humans entered the sharks' world in a big way. Since then the two things threatening sharks and their relatives are fishing and human-caused global climate change. Worldwide, fishing (both directed and incidental) is and will continue to be the greatest threat.

In the northeast Pacific Ocean, as in the rest of the world's oceans, the assessment and management of elasmobranchs present problems for researchers and managers because of the life-history characteristics of these species. Their extreme longevity, slow growth, late maturity, long gestation period and low fecundity make the populations slow to recover from over-exploitation.

This is not to say that some shark and skate populations cannot be fished in a sustainable manner, but we need to fully understand elasmobranch biology and ecology to sustainably manage fishery encounters. While we have made some progress in understanding the effects of fishing (direct and incidental) of sharks and their relatives, there remain pressing research questions about how to protect elasmobranchs, including those found off the coast of British Columbia.

Gaining a thorough biological and ecological understanding would require improved sampling and assessment techniques. We need accurate catch statistics, data about population sizes and their geographic limits, and estimates of life-history parameters. In the area of fisheries reporting, we need more accurate catch reporting (especially of discarded fish), better species identification, and research to estimate mortality rates for fish discarded at sea. We need genetic studies and tagging studies to determine the boundaries between distinct populations and map movement and migratory behaviour patterns. We particularly need to improve our knowledge of where pupping or nursery grounds are, how long juveniles stay near the shore and when they subsequently migrate to deepwater habitat. And we also need increased research on the basic life-history factors of fecundity, age, mortality and growth. For good fisheries management, we need more work on developing good methods to assess population status and trends for elasmobranchs, including methods that can deal with very little or inaccurate data and methods that include information about the environment.

Additionally, in coming decades and centuries, global climate change (including increased temperatures) will increase habitat degradation and destruction, ocean acidification and increased bioaccumulation of pollutants. These changes in turn will alter the ecosystems that sharks, skates, rays and chimeras are an integral part of, although there is little information to what extent elasmobranchs, which are highly adaptable, will be affected. It is likely that the greatest impact will be on species with restricted ranges and those that depend on special nearshore habitats for shelter, food or nursery areas. However, highly migratory species could also be affected. Rising temperatures may cause their distribution to shift toward the poles or to deeper waters. In addition, given the strong affinity of female sharks of some species for specific water temperatures, a warming climate may induce a major shift in spawning or nursery grounds. All of these challenges will need to be addressed if we are to protect these fascinating fishes for future generations. Ultimately, improvements in the management and conservation of shark populations will come by developing sound, science-based fisheries-management practices both for fisheries that target sharks and those that catch sharks incidentally.

Key to the Species

We use taxonomic keys to identify unknown fishes. Identification keys offer mostly paired choices. Select the choice that best fits your specimen (for example, either **1A** or **1B** to start), and continue to additional choices or a species account as the key suggests. If the final image and description do not match what you captured or sighted, then the number in brackets after each number choice allows you to backtrack in the guide to check other options. This guide contains as few technical terms as possible so that anyone, specialist or not, will be able to use it. See diagrams 2 and 3 and the glossary for illustrations and terminology. The key is not meant to indicate the true relationships among fishes. This key is a modification of keys by other authors.

1A   body cylindrical in cross-section; pectoral fins not integrated into the profile of the head; gills on the side of the body; eyes on the side of the head; pectoral fins mostly or entirely behind the gill slits: **GO TO 2**

1B   body flattened in cross-section; pectoral fins broad and extending forward of the gill slits; pectoral fins merged with the head or separated by a groove but still forming a continuous edge; gills ventral or usually ventrolateral (that is, hidden by the pectoral fins); eyes on top of the head: **GO TO 16**

2A (1A)   elongated, tapering body with a long filamentous, whip-like tail; single enlarged fin spine in front of the first dorsal fin; second dorsal fin long and low with no spine; skin smooth and scales absent; anal fin merged with the caudal fin; incisor-like tooth plates in a small mouth: *Hydrolagus colliei*—White-spotted ratfish (page 175)

2B (1A)   body tapering, but tail not filamentous and whip-like; both dorsal fins have fin spines or dorsal fins lack spines; scales present; multiple and separate teeth line the jaws and are not fused into tooth plates: **GO TO 3**

3A (2B)   one dorsal fin present and set well back along the body; six or seven gill slits present: **GO TO 4**

3B (2B)   two dorsal fins present; five gill slits present: **GO TO 5**

4A (3A)   six gill slits present; lower jaw with broad teeth having eight to twelve cusplets; body uniformly grey brown; lower lobe of the caudal fin broad with slightly concave margin (edge): *Hexanchus griseus*—Bluntnose sixgill shark (page 51)

4B (3A)   seven gill slits present; lower jaw with broad teeth having five or six cusplets; body with dark spots or blotches; lower lobe of the caudal fin with prominent concave margin: *Notorynchus cepedianus*—Broadnose sevengill shark (page 55)

5A (3B)   anal fin present: **GO TO 6**

5B (3B)   anal fin absent: **GO TO 14**

6A (5A)   stiff tail as long as the body; teeth small without cusplets; gill slits small relative to body depth; crescent-shaped pectoral fins far larger than the dorsal fin: *Alopias vulpinus*—Common thresher shark (page 97)

6B (5A)   tail far shorter than the body; teeth variable with or without cusplets; gill slits moderate to large relative to body depth; pectoral fin usually not much larger than the first dorsal fin: **GO TO 7**

7A (6B) small and soft bodied; first dorsal fin positioned far back along the body level with pelvic fins; anal fin with straight to convex margin and much larger than the first dorsal fin: *Apristurus brunneus*—Brown catshark (page 101)

7B (6B) first dorsal fin positioned ahead of the pelvic fins; larger body; anal fin with a concave margin and smaller than the first dorsal fin: **GO TO 8**

8A (7B) gill slits less than half the body depth; caudal fin lobes strongly asymmetrical; caudal peduncle without laterally expanded keels (raised areas): **GO TO 9**

8B (7B) gill slits greater than half the body depth and even extending toward the dorsal midline; caudal fin lobes nearly symmetrical; caudal peduncle with laterally expanded keels: **GO TO 11**

9A (8A) head laterally expanded into a hammer shape: *Sphyrna zygaena*—Smooth hammerhead shark (page 111)

9B (8A) head conical: **GO TO 10**

10A (9B) pectoral fin long and sickle shaped; the notched tip of the upper lobe of caudal fin not greatly enlarged relative to the rest of the lobe; anal fin larger than the second dorsal; first dorsal with strongly concave trailing margin: *Prionace glauca*—Blue shark (page 107)

10B (9B) pectoral fin not enlarged and about the same length as the first dorsal fin; the notched tip of the upper lobe of the caudal fin large relative to the rest of the lobe; anal fin about the same size as the second dorsal fin; first dorsal fin triangular with nearly straight to slightly concave trailing margin: *Galeorhinus galeus*—Tope (soupfin) shark (page 103)

11A (8B)   gill slits huge and extend onto the dorsal surface of the body; gill rakers are like bristles; teeth minute; large body with enlarged conical snout: *Cetorhinus maximus*—Basking shark (page 91)

11B (8B)   gill slits not expanded onto the dorsal surface of body; teeth large and pointy; snout conical; body large and spindle shaped: **GO TO 12**

12A (11B)   broad triangular teeth in the upper jaw; upper jaw teeth with serrated edges; stiletto-shaped teeth in the lower jaw; dark spot behind the base of the pectoral fin; a grey back to white belly: *Carcharodon carcharias*—Great white shark (page 81)

12B (11B)   teeth along the upper and lower jaws smooth edged and stiletto shaped; no dark spot behind the base of the pectoral fin: **GO TO 13**

13A (12B)   body evenly coloured steel blue grey with a white belly; sharp and acutely pointed snout; first dorsal fin positioned behind the base of the pectoral fin; teeth without lateral cusplets: *Isurus oxyrinchus*—Shortfin mako shark (page 85)

13B (12B)   body sooty grey with a white belly; dark spots and blotches along the lower flank and belly; snout short and bluntly conical; origin of the first dorsal fin is level with the base of the pectoral fin; teeth have small lateral cusplets: *Lamna ditropis*—Salmon shark (page 87)

14A (5B)   dorsal fins without spines; moderate to large flabby body; upper and lower jaws with dissimilar teeth; snout blunt and broadly rounded: *Somniosus pacificus*—Pacific sleeper shark (page 67)

14B (5B) both dorsal fins have spines; small- to moderate-sized body; teeth similar along the upper and lower jaws: **GO TO 15**

15A (14B) teeth small and when combined form a continuous blade-like cutting surface; first dorsal fin larger than the second dorsal fin; no photophores (light-emitting organs) in the skin: *Squalus suckleyi*—Pacific spiny dogfish (page 61)

15B (14B) teeth have a median cusp and one to two lateral cusplets; dorsal fins equal in size; photophores (light-emitting organs) present in the skin: Etmopteridae—Lanternsharks (genera and species yet to be identified) (page 71)

16A (1B) pectoral fin separated from the head; caudal fin distinct with two lobes; mouth at the end of the snout; gill slits ventrolateral and usually hidden by the pectoral fins: *Squatina californica*—Pacific angel shark (page 75)

16B (1B) pectoral fin fused to the margin of the head; caudal fin with two lobes that are reduced or absent; mouth just below the snout; gill slits on the ventral surface: **GO TO 17**

17A (16B) tail filamentous and whip-like and caudal fin absent; long stinging spine at the base of the tail along the dorsal midline: *Pteroplatytrygon violacea*—Pelagic stingray (page 167)

17B (16B) tail not filamentous and whip-like; caudal fin present but may be reduced; long stinging spine absent from the base of the tail: **GO TO 18**

18A (17B) skin smooth; body soft and flabby; pectoral-fin margins create a rounded to oval-shaped disc; first dorsal fin larger than the second; caudal fin well developed and vaguely heart shaped: *Tetronarce californica*—Pacific torpedo (electric) ray (page 163)

18B (17B) dorsal surface of the body with enlarged thorns; caudal fin reduced to a fringe around the tail tip; dorsal fins about the same size; pectoral disc roughly rhomboid; body and skin are usually firm: **GO TO 19**

19A (18B) snout rigid and stiff: **GO TO 20**

19B (18B) snout flabby and flexible: **GO TO 24**

20A (19A) scapular thorns present; median thorn row present from the head to the dorsal fins: **GO TO 21**

20B (19A) scapular thorns absent; nuchal thorns separate from the tail thorns: **GO TO 22**

21A (20A) snout short with median cluster of thornlets on the tip; disc wider than it is long; median thorn row on the tail flanked by enlarged thornlets: *Amblyraja badia*—Broad skate (page 147)

21B (20A) snout short without median cluster of thornlets; disc about as wide as long; dorsal surface and much of underside of the disc covered with star-shaped prickles; multiple rows of thorns converge on the median thorn row from the mid-back to the first dorsal fin: *Raja stellulata*—Starry skate (page 157)

22A (20B) snout extremely long and acutely pointed for most of its length; pelvic fins with deep notch; one or two nuchal thorns; leading edge of the disc significantly concave: *Raja rhina*—Longnose skate (page 153)

22B (20B) snout moderately long and acutely pointed only near the tip; leading edge of the disc not significantly concave: **GO TO 23**

23A (22B) disc with angular lateral margins; one nuchal thorn present; weak notch in the trailing edge of the pelvic fin; dark spots (ocelli) on the disc surrounded by concentric patterns of light spots: *Beringraja binoculata*—Big skate (page 149)

23B (22B) disc with rounded lateral margins; up to three nuchal thorns present; pelvic fins with deep notch in the trailing edge; dark spots on disc not surrounded by light spots: *Raja inornata*—California skate (page 161)

24A (19B) scapular thorns present: **GO TO 25**

24B (19B) scapular thorns absent: **GO TO 27**

25A (24A) orbital thorns present: *Bathyraja parmifera*—Alaska skate (page 137)

25B (24A) orbital thorns absent: **GO TO 26**

26A (25B) preorbital snout length more than 75 per cent of the head length: *Bathyraja aleutica*—Aleutian skate (page 125)

26B (25B) preorbital snout length less than 75 per cent of the head length; thorns in a continuous single row on the back: *Bathyraja kincaidii*—Sandpaper skate (page 127)

26C (25B) preorbital snout length less than 75 per cent of the head length; thorns in a non-continuous single row on the back: *Bathyraja interrupta*—Bering skate (page 133)

27A (24B) denticles across the ventral surface: **GO TO 28**

27B (24B) no denticles across the ventral surface: **GO TO 29**

28A (27A) one to five nuchal to mid-dorsal thorns present; prominent row of median thorns from the pelvic region to the first dorsal fin: *Bathyraja abyssicola*—Deepsea skate (page 123)

28B (27A) no nuchal or mid-dorsal thorns: *Bathyraja spinosissima*—Pacific white skate (page 145)

29A (27B) nuchal thorns present (occasionally absent); light crescent-shaped patches next to the middle of the eyes; ventral surface uniformly dark: *Bathyraja minispinosa*—Whitebrow skate (page 143)

29B (27B) nuchal thorns absent; no crescent-shaped white patches next to the middle of the eyes: **GO TO 30**

30A (29B) well-developed median thorns from the head to the first dorsal fin: *Bathyraja lindbergi*—Commander skate (page 141)

30B (29B) no mid-dorsal thorns on the disc; thorns begin over the pelvic region: **GO TO 31**

31A (30B) ventral surface uniformly dark: *Bathyraja trachura*—Roughtail skate (page 135)

31B (30B) central part of the ventral surface and the anterior parts of the underside of the pelvic fins white: *Bathyraja microtrachys*—Fine-spined skate (page 131)

Species Descriptions

Contrary to the public misconception that BC waters are devoid of sharks and other shark-like fishes, elasmobranchs off the Pacific coast of Canada are in fact quite diverse, and in some cases, abundant. Ten orders of the class Chondrichthyes are recognized worldwide: eight of these contain the "typical" sharks, one comprises skates and rays and one is made up of chimeras. Of these ten orders, seven are represented in BC waters: the orders of skates and rays and chimeras, and five out of the seven orders of "typical" sharks. BC waters contain 33 chondrichthyan species: 15 species of shark from 12 families, 15 species of skate from 2 families, 2 species of ray from 2 families, and 1 species of chimera.

Of the 17 chondrichthyan families in BC waters, the family Arhynchobatidae (softnose skates) is the most species-rich with 10 species represented. The next most species-rich family is the Rajidae (hardnose skates) with 5 species, and then the Lamnidae (mackerel sharks) with 3 species. One family, the Hexanchidae, has 2 representative species, and the remaining 13 families are represented by a single species each. In total, BC waters contain 33 chondrichthyan species.

Species range in size from the small brown catshark, which has an average total length of 40 to 50 centimetres, to the second-largest fish in the world, the basking shark, which can reach sizes of approximately 12 to 15 metres in total length. Based on catch records, the Pacific spiny dogfish, the longnose skate and the big skate are the most abundant elasmobranchs in British Columbia. There are at least three species known from only a single specimen each.

Previous attempts to compile lists of sharks, skates and rays that occur in British Columbia have been complicated by erroneous records, species misidentification and coding errors in databases. A compounding factor with misidentification of skates and rays is that the taxonomy has been changed as scientific knowledge improved, and sometimes this has caused confusion between historic and current names for some species.

Here we follow current taxonomy and standardized common names, and list only confirmed documented records of chondrichthyans in BC waters, or just outside provincial boundaries. Hopefully, this summary dismisses all previous erroneous reports.

IMAGE 7
Big skate swimming on the surface after being tagged during a Fisheries and Oceans Canada skate survey in Queen Charlotte Sound. PHOTO: G. MCFARLANE.

Sharks

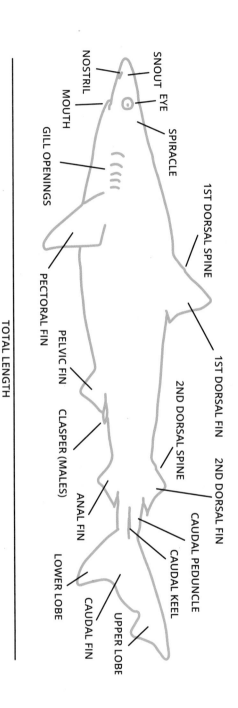

SNOUT

EYE

NOSTRIL

MOUTH

GILL OPENINGS

SPIRACLE

PECTORAL FIN

PELVIC FIN

CLASPER (MALES)

ANAL FIN

LOWER LOBE

CAUDAL FIN

UPPER LOBE

CAUDAL KEEL

CAUDAL PEDUNCLE

2ND DORSAL FIN

2ND DORSAL SPINE

1ST DORSAL FIN

1ST DORSAL SPINE

TOTAL LENGTH

DIAGRAM 2
Morphological terminology of sharks used in this handbook.

48   SHARKS

Order Hexanchiformes (Cow sharks and frill sharks)

The cow and frill sharks are one of the most primitive groups of modern-day sharks. They have six or seven paired gill slits (compared to five in other sharks), a single dorsal fin set close to the tail, an anal fin, and eyes without the protective nictitating membranes.

Species in this order are separated into two families, the Chlamydoselachidae (frill sharks) and the Hexanchidae (cow sharks). Frill sharks are long, eel-like sharks, which differ in many ways from the cow sharks and will most likely be moved to their own order in the near future. Only cow sharks are present in BC waters.

Cow sharks are stout and stocky in build. They are a small family of sharks consisting of only four living species, two of which are present in BC waters. They are found worldwide, and have adapted themselves to a broad range of habitats from nearshore coastal waters to deeper open ocean waters of over 2,500 metres.

Family: Hexanchidae (cow sharks)
Fusiform body shape; six or seven gill slits; single dorsal fin set far back on the body

Hexanchus griseus (bluntnose sixgill shark)
Six paired gill slits; long narrow teeth in upper jaw; large comb-like or saw-like teeth in lower jaw with 8 to 12 cusplets

Notorynchus cepedianus (broadnose sevengill shark)
Seven paired gill slits; long narrow teeth in upper jaw, large comb-like or saw-like teeth in lower jaw with five to six cusplets

IMAGE 8

A bluntnose sixgill shark ready to be released back in the Strait of Georgia, tagged with a satellite tag that stores temperature and depth observations. Advances in technology have made it possible to gain insight to shark behaviour, habitat usage and distribution.

PHOTO: J. KING.

Quick Bite

Sharks have a superhero ability: electroreception. Small gel-filled organs called *ampullae of Lorenzini* cover a shark's head near the snout area. Sharks use these organs to detect weak electric fields at short ranges, allowing them to notice hidden predator or prey and to hunt at night.

Bluntnose sixgill shark

Hexanchus griseus
FAMILY Hexanchidae (cow sharks)

CONSERVATION STATUS
SC Special Concern (Canada's Species at Risk Act)
SC Special Concern (COSEWIC)
NT Near Threatened (IUCN Red List)

DESCRIPTION
The obvious defining feature is the presence of six gill openings and a distinctly blunt snout. An additional feature that helps to identify the bluntnose sixgill shark is the single dorsal fin placed well back on the body (as compared to the usual two dorsal fins for most shark species in British Columbia). The bluntnose sixgill shark is one of our largest elasmobranchs, with a recorded maximum size of 4.8 m. Their backs are brown or blackish grey, and their bellies are white. The caudal fin is large, about one-third of the total length. The upper lobe of the caudal fin is much larger than the lower lobe, and is notched. These sharks have long narrow teeth along the upper jaw and large comb-like teeth along the lower jaw.

RANGE
Worldwide, mainly in temperate and cold oceans. Off the west coast of North America, they are found from California up through to Alaska. In

IMAGE 9 **Bluntnose sixgill shark** (*Hexanchus griseus*)
Typically a deepwater inhabitant. British Columbia
is one of the few places in the world where juveniles
occupy shallow waters, making them accessible to
scuba divers. PHOTO: A. MURCH.

British Columbia, adults are found in deeper waters along the west coast
of Vancouver Island and Haida Gwaii as well as Queen Charlotte Sound.
Juveniles are common in shallow waters and in bays and inlets along the
west coast of Vancouver Island and in the Strait of Georgia.

GENERAL BIOLOGY

The maximum age estimated for the bluntnose sixgill shark is 80 years.
The maximum verified reported length is 4.8 m. Although lengths
greater than 5.0 m should not be unexpected, claims of specimens over
8 m are considered false.

This species is sexually dimorphic with females growing larger than
males, and males, as with other elasmobranchs, having obvious external
claspers. Length at maturity for females has been reported elsewhere in
the world at 4.2–4.8 m. However, in the Strait of Georgia, a female 4.0 m

long carrying 5 pups was found washed up on shore. For males, length at maturity is known primarily from South African waters at 3.1m. Age of maturity is estimated to be 18–35 for females and 11–14 for males.

Although courtship and mating have not been observed, they are thought to take place in deep water. Seasonal appearance of scars on the females suggests that the males bite the females near the gills, pectoral fins and flank. Bluntnose sixgill sharks are ovoviviparous, meaning the young hatch within the female's body before being released. Females have a 2-year reproductive cycle with an estimated 12- to 24-month gestation. The bluntnose sixgill shark is one of the most fecund species of elasmobranch. However, the litter size is known from only three credible accounts of 47, 51 and 70 pups (with pups from 61 to 73 cm in size). An unverified report of a single specimen with 108 pups exists from a fisherman in France at the turn of the 20th century.

ECOLOGY

They are deepwater sharks, typically living in waters as deep as 2,500 m. However, Vancouver Island is one of the only locations in the world where the bluntnose sixgill shark routinely inhabits shallow, nearshore waters. Tagging of juvenile bluntnose sixgill sharks in the Strait of Georgia suggests that they remain in the area until they mature and then migrate offshore. Even in shallow, nearshore waters, tagged juvenile sharks still preferred deep water (>200 m), but they showed interesting daily and seasonal patterns in the depth they occupied—with shallow depths selected at night and in summer. Association with a large range of temperatures, and the synchrony in daily and seasonal patterns suggest that their vertical behaviour is influenced by local foraging opportunities and not by thermoregulation.

The bluntnose sixgill shark is considered to be a lethargic, non-aggressive shark. They are generalist feeders primarily foraging nocturnally on a wide variety of prey items including cephalopods and crustaceans. Bony fishes predominate in the diet—for example, Pacific hake, Pacific herring, flatfish, cod, salmon and rockfish—but they also feed on sharks (Pacific spiny dogfish) and skates. Sixgills also feed on the carrion of marine mammals including porpoises (Phocoenidae), dolphins (Delphinidae) and sea lions. Their deepwater existence and large size probably limit their potential as prey for sea lions, but they are likely taken by offshore killer whales here in British Columbia.

USE

The bluntnose sixgill shark has been the focus of at least three known directed fisheries in Canadian waters. The first was in the early 1920s around the waters of Mayne Island in the southern Strait of Georgia. The focus of the fishery was on "mudshark" skins used to make shark leathers. The success of this venture in terms of the sharks caught and duration of the fishery is unknown; however, newspaper articles from the time report an experimental fishery capturing 357 sharks over a 24-day period.

The second directed fishery for these sharks took place between 1937 and 1946 throughout British Columbia. This fishery primarily targeted the livers of the sharks, which were processed for vitamin A. Landing statistics for this species did not appear in government records until 1942, when 276 tonnes of bluntnose sixgill shark liver was marketed in British Columbia.

The third directed fishery was an experimental fishery off the west coast of Vancouver Island in 1993 and 1994. The fishery successfully marketed the bluntnose sixgill shark as "snow shark," and its flesh was highly valued for human consumption. The experimental fishery was discontinued when it became known that the major component of the catch was juvenile sharks. Beginning in the late 1970s and 1980s, interest by divers led to the development of a lucrative dive industry to view bluntnose sixgill sharks in British Columbia at locations where they occur in shallow waters. This attracted divers from around the world. More recently, this activity has decreased due to changes in shark distribution resulting from environmental changes (increased water temperatures).

Quick Bite

Sharks predate dinosaurs by over 200 million years. However, the "modern" sharks in this book appeared around 100 million years ago.

Broadnose sevengill shark

Notorynchus cepedianus
FAMILY Hexanchidae (cow sharks)

CONSERVATION STATUS
Not Listed (Canada's Species at Risk Act)
Data Deficient (COSEWIC)
Data Deficient (IUCN Red List)

DESCRIPTION
Like the other cow sharks, broadnose sevengill sharks are easily identifiable by the number of gill openings (seven) and the presence of one dorsal fin. Sevengill sharks are grey to reddish brown with numerous small black spots. Their colouring is paler on their belly. The caudal fin is similar to bluntnose sixgill sharks: a large, notched upper lobe, but with more curvature to the edge of the lower lobe. Their nose is broad and blunt. They have long narrow teeth in their upper jaw, and large comb-like or saw-like teeth in their lower jaw.

RANGE
Broadnose sevengill sharks are common in global temperate waters. In the north Pacific they are found from the Gulf of California up to northern British Columbia and from Japan to China. In BC waters their distribution and occurrence are not well known, since they live in shallower water than is covered by most fisheries or research surveys.

They have been encountered in the Strait of Georgia, off the southwest coast of Vancouver Island and in Hecate Strait.

GENERAL BIOLOGY

The maximum size is 3 m, though unconfirmed reports suggest a maximum size of 4 m. There are no estimates of ages for broadnose sevengill sharks. Males mature between the sizes of 1.5 and 1.8 m, and females mature at larger sizes, 2.2–2.5 m.

They are ovoviviparous, meaning the young hatch within the female's body before being released. Gestation period is estimated to be about 12 months, but females give birth only every 2 years and have litters of up to 86 pups. The pups are born at sizes of 35–45 cm and double this size within the first 2 years. Pupping occurs in shallow, coastal areas in late spring and early summer.

IMAGE 10 Broadnose sevengill shark (*Notorynchus cepedianus*) Easily identified by the number of gill openings. PHOTO: A. MURCH.

ECOLOGY

They are the only shallow-water cow sharks, living on the bottom at depths to 50 m. They can be found in waters less than 1 m deep. They commonly move into bays with high tide, moving out again at low tide. Unlike bluntnose sixgill sharks, broadnose sevengill sharks are highly active and are considered potentially dangerous. They feed on fish such as Pacific salmon (*Oncorhynchus* spp.; the name "Pacific salmon" includes various species) and Pacific herring, other sharks (including Pacific spiny dogfish, tope sharks and Pacific angel sharks), as well as large skates. They also eat marine mammals, including seals and dolphins. They are typically solitary hunters when preying on fish; however, they have been observed to hunt in packs when attacking other sharks and marine mammals. The only confirmed predator of broadnose sevengill sharks is the great white shark.

USE

Broadnose sevengill sharks were caught incidentally in the BC dogfish-liver fishery in the 1930s and 40s, when the livers were used as a source of oil for vitamin A and lubrication. Countries such as China harvest broadnose sevengill sharks and use their skin as a source of leather. In the United States, there is growing interest from recreational anglers in pursuing this active shark. Its flesh is apparently good to eat. There are no directed commercial or recreational fisheries in British Columbia, though they are occasionally caught incidentally.

Quick Bite
Sharks, skates and rays have skeletons made from cartilage, similar to your nose and ears.

Order Squaliformes (Dogfish sharks)

The dogfish sharks are the second-largest order of sharks worldwide. They are a diverse group that contain the smallest as well as some very large shark species. Sharks from this order are characterized by two small to moderate dorsal fins (usually but not always preceded by a spine), no anal fin and no nictitating membrane to protect the eyes.

These sharks are variable in shape and size, and are found in marine habitats worldwide. Three species occur in BC waters.

Family: Squalidae (dogfish sharks)
Teeth small and flattened, forming a continuous cutting edge; first dorsal fin larger than the second, with both preceded by a spine

Squalus suckleyi (Pacific spiny dogfish)
Teeth in upper and lower jaws are small, blade-like and flattened forming a continuous cutting edge; prominent fin spine preceding each dorsal fin

Family: Somniosidae (sleeper sharks)
Moderate- to large-bodied sharks; large, robust, flaccid body; dorsal fins with no fin spines, low and equal in size; teeth dissimilar in upper and lower jaws

Somniosus pacificus (Pacific sleeper shark)
Upper teeth have a single, slender, erect smooth-edged cusp, and lower teeth have a short, strongly oblique cusp; snout long and rounded; body large, robust and flaccid

Family: Etmopteridae (lanternsharks)
Body small and cylindrical in shape; photophores present on lower surface; dorsal fins equal in size and preceded by spines; teeth similar in both jaws with a median cusp flanked on each side by one or two cusplets

Genera and species yet to be identified.

Quick Bite
Some sharks, such as the Pacific spiny dogfish and the basking shark, can be pregnant for about two years. That's a lot of pickles and ice cream.

Pacific spiny dogfish

Squalus suckleyi
FAMILY Squalidae (dogfish sharks)

CONSERVATION STATUS
Not Listed (Canada's Species at Risk Act)
SC Special Concern (COSEWIC)
LC Least Concern (IUCN Red List)

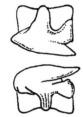

DESCRIPTION

The Pacific spiny dogfish is distinguished by the spines present just in front of each dorsal fin. The snout is relatively pointed, and the body is fairly slender. The teeth in both the upper and lower jaws have obliquely angled crowns, which combine to form a continuous cutting edge. This shark is greyish brown above, fading to a white belly. Along the flank and back are prominent, irregular white spots, which may disappear with age. The Pacific spiny dogfish was previously considered the same species as the spiny dogfish that occurs in the Atlantic (*Squalus acanthias*), but modern genetic population studies indicate that the Pacific fish represent a distinct species.

RANGE

Pacific spiny dogfish are found throughout the north Pacific. They are very abundant in waters off British Columbia, with a large portion of

IMAGE 11   Pacific spiny dogfish (*Squalus suckleyi*)
Ubiquitous and the most abundant shark in our
waters. This shark has sustained fisheries since the
late 1800s. PHOTO: A. MURCH.

their northeast Pacific core range found here. There are high abundances
in the Strait of Georgia, on the continental shelf of the west coast of
Vancouver Island, and in Queen Charlotte Sound, Hecate Strait and
Dixon Entrance. Tagging studies in British Columbia show that some of
these sharks migrate across the Pacific, travelling from British Columbia
to Japan. Some sharks also make large north-south migrations, with a
few sharks travelling from the west coast of Vancouver Island northward
to the Aleutian Islands or southward to Baja California.

GENERAL BIOLOGY
As a result of their low metabolic rate, Pacific spiny dogfish in the
northeast Pacific grow exceptionally slowly. Adults reach sizes of
approximately 1 m, although the maximum recorded size is 1.6 m. The
maximum estimated age is 105 years. Females mature at about 35 years,
or a size of about 95 cm in total length. Males mature at a smaller size
and age—70 cm and 20 years, respectively.

In the northeast Pacific, breeding occurs during the late fall and early winter. Development is ovoviviparous. Encapsulated fertilized eggs remain in the oviducts for nearly 2 years, a verified gestation period in a shark unmatched by any other species in the animal kingdom with the exception of the Indian elephant. During gestation, the shells dissolve, and the free embryos are nourished by yolk material, which they gradually deplete until they reach a full-term size averaging between 26 and 27 cm. To protect the mother, the embryos develop a rubbery tip on each dorsal spine. In BC waters, fecundity in the spiny dogfish varies from 2 to 16 pups, and is highly dependent on the size of the mother, with larger females bearing more young. The average number of pups born ranges from 6 to 7.

ECOLOGY

Pacific spiny dogfish are found as aggregations at depths from surface waters down to 1,200 m and in areas from intertidal zones to well offshore. They can tolerate a wide range of salinities including estuarine waters. Pacific spiny dogfish less than 15 years old and approximately 60 cm or less occupy mainly pelagic waters, albeit at all depths of the water column. Older Pacific spiny dogfish leave the pelagic habitat and spend most of their time on or near the bottom. Adults segregate by sex, with females occupying deeper waters than males. Additionally, there is seasonal selection of habitat depths with movement into shallower waters in summer, either onto banks or shallower portions of the continental slope. These seasonal movements likely are a reflection of prey distribution and feeding opportunities.

Young Pacific spiny dogfish are born as miniature replicas of their parents and are released within the water column in waters overlying depths of 165–350 m. They almost immediately begin feeding on a variety of small invertebrates. As growth progresses and juveniles become bottom dwellers, their diet gradually shifts to fish. Adult Pacific spiny

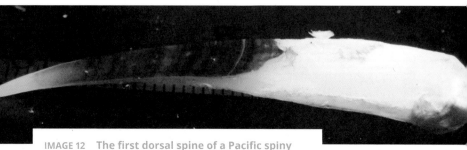

IMAGE 12   **The first dorsal spine of a Pacific spiny dogfish under ultraviolet light**
Fisheries and Oceans Canada researchers used the antibiotic oxytetracycline to provide a time mark on the spine (visible here as a yellow band). Years later, when the shark was recaptured, researchers could validate their method of estimating age since the number of dark bands after the time mark corresponded to the number of years that the shark was at liberty.
PHOTO: G. MCFARLANE / M. SMITH.

dogfish are opportunistic feeders, eating invertebrate prey such as squid, jellyfish, crabs and krill (euphausiids) and fish prey such as Pacific herring, Pacific salmon, flatfish, capelin and eulachon. The dominance of prey items in their diet can be different between ecosystems, with Pacific spiny dogfish eating mainly Pacific herring in the Strait of Georgia, and mainly krill off the west coast of Vancouver Island. Although commonly viewed by fishers as ravaging other commercial species, digestion is a slow process in Pacific spiny dogfish, with an observed time between feeding events of 2 weeks or more in BC waters. Pacific spiny dogfish are eaten by predators including large bony fishes such as lingcod and sablefish, other shark species such as bluntnose sixgill sharks, and marine mammals such as killer whales and Steller sea lions.

Quick Bite
Why the name *dogfish?* It's simple—because they bite!

USE

First Nations have used Pacific spiny dogfish for at least 4,000 years. Some used it as a source of food, mainly when other sources of food were scarce. Many cultures rendered oil from the liver and flesh for use as medicine, a food flavouring and, like white-spotted ratfish oil, as a general hair tonic. The oil was used to treat the inner and outer surfaces of canoes, to protect and polish wood, and in some cultures, to paint. Besides using the liver oil, dogfish spines were used as awls and needles, and the skin was used as a form of sandpaper.

The commercial fishery for Pacific spiny dogfish in Canada's Pacific waters has a long and varied history dating back to 1870. There have been several major fisheries for Pacific spiny dogfish that have mirrored changes in the market demands. In the late 1800s to early 1900s, the liver oil was used for industrial lubrication, lighting and fertilizer, and in the mid-1900s the oil was used as a source of vitamin A. Following the liver fishery, this species was considered a nuisance because of its large population coupled with the lack of a market. From 1958 to 1962, the Canadian government conducted a number of eradication programs. These programs were unsuccessful and were halted in 1962.

In the mid-1970s, new import markets in Europe and Asia spurred the development of a successful food fish fishery. This fishery remained relatively large and stable for the next 30 years. Since 2006, as a result of a new management system and reduced market demand, commercial fishing for Pacific spiny dogfish has declined dramatically. Even so, the Pacific spiny dogfish continues to be the shark species of greatest commercial importance on the Pacific coast. It is important to note that the declines in Pacific spiny dogfish landings at the end of each major fishery era have not been attributed solely to declines in abundance; each time there was also a decline in demand as alternate sources for the products of the fishery became available.

Quick Bite

Sharks live in all of the world's oceans, and a few are also found in fresh water. In British Columbia, Pacific spiny dogfish can tolerate brackish water (mixed salt and fresh water) and are known to enter river mouths in search of food.

Pacific sleeper shark

Somniosus pacificus
FAMILY Somniosidae (sleeper sharks)

CONSERVATION STATUS
Not Listed (Canada's Species at Risk Act)
Not Assessed (COSEWIC)
Data Deficient (IUCN Red List)

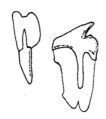

DESCRIPTION
Pacific sleeper sharks are a uniform blackish brown to grey and have a bristly, rough skin. They have large stout cylindrical bodies with a short, rounded snout. The dorsal fins are placed far back on the body and are almost equal in size. They lack an anal fin, and the caudal fin is short and broad. Pacific sleeper sharks have a small mouth with spike-like teeth in the upper jaw and broad teeth with oblique cusps in the lower jaw. This dental arrangement is suited for grasping and sawing hunks of flesh from large prey.

RANGE
Pacific sleeper sharks are found in the northwest and northeast Pacific. In the northeast Pacific they range from the Bering Sea southward to Baja California. In BC waters, they are frequently encountered in deeper waters off the west coasts of Vancouver Island and Haida Gwaii, as well as Queen Charlotte Sound.

IMAGE 13 Pacific sleeper shark (*Somniosus pacificus*)
In offshore waters of British Columbia, these sharks are
preyed upon by the killer whale (*Orcinus orca*) (the offshore
ecotype). PHOTO: A. MURCH.

GENERAL BIOLOGY

Pacific sleeper sharks are one of the biggest shark species, with the largest
verified record of 4.4 m but with an unconfirmed record (estimated from
photographs) of 7.0 m. Females are estimated to mature at 3.7 m, and
males by at least 4.0 m. There are currently no estimates of longevity for
Pacific sleeper sharks.

Pacific sleeper shark reproduction is yolk-sac viviparous, although
no pregnant females have ever been found. The gestation period is
unknown but is possibly 2 years or more. Litter sizes are thought to be
about 10 pups, and size at birth is estimated to be 40–65 cm.

ECOLOGY

Pacific sleeper sharks are a deepwater shark, but in northern areas
they can be found in shallow waters, coming near the surface at night.
They prefer deep, colder waters and have been recorded at depths of
2,000 m. Because they live in this deep, frigid environment, Pacific

sleeper shark livers do not contain squalene (used for buoyancy); the low temperatures would solidify it into a dense mass that would provide little buoyancy and no energy source for when feeding conditions were poor. Instead, the liver contains low-density compounds that maintain their fluidity, even at the lowest temperatures the sharks encounter. Like other deepwater sharks, they have relatively little urea in their skins, but have high concentrations of nitrogenous waste products in their tissues to stabilize the proteins in their cells against the crushing pressures encountered at depth, and to increase their buoyancy.

Pacific sleeper sharks are thought to be both predators and scavengers. They are slow moving but can glide through the water with little body movement, making them successful predators because they make so little noise. Diet studies in Alaska showed they feed on a variety of pelagic and bottom prey including flatfish, walleye pollock, Pacific salmon, rockfishes, shrimp, octopus, squid, crabs and marine snails. Larger sharks have been found with marine mammals (harbour seals and sea lions) in their guts. It is believed that the fast-moving pelagic fishes such as salmon, as well as the marine mammals, are picked up as carrion by these slow-moving sharks. The only confirmed predator of sleeper sharks is the offshore ecotype of killer whales, which has been observed feeding on sleeper sharks off British Columbia.

USE

There is no commercial use of the Pacific sleeper shark. It is taken as bycatch in several fisheries (trawl and longline) and is usually discarded. Off British Columbia, small sharks are often captured in traps set on the bottom for sablefish.

Quick Bite

Sharks are all about teeth. They generally have a front row of about 45 to 50 teeth, but they also have as many as seven replacement rows behind, ready to move into place if a tooth is damaged or falls out. This means that a shark might go through as many as 30,000 teeth in a lifetime.

Lanternsharks

Etmopteridae

FAMILY Etmopteridae (lanternsharks)

Lanternsharks are small, slender sharks. They have two dorsal fins, each preceded by a spine. Many lanternsharks have photophores (light-emitting organs) in the skin of their bellies, hence their name. Lanternsharks are among the world's smallest shark species, with most species less than 100 cm long, and many less than 50 cm long. They are deepwater sharks, occupying waters on continental slopes and open ocean.

There are two species of lanternsharks that are found in the central or eastern north Pacific: the Pacific black dogfish, also known as combtooth dogfish (*Centroscyllium nigrum*) and the Hawaiian lanternshark (*Etmopterus villosus*). The Hawaiian lanternshark is generally found off the Hawaiian Islands, whereas the Pacific black dogfish is found off California and sporadically in waters in the central and eastern north Pacific. Lanternsharks were encountered by commercial trawl fisheries operating in continental-slope waters off Vancouver Island in 1991 and 1995. The sharks were identified by trained at-sea observers, who noted that the sharks had spines in front of each dorsal fin but were definitely not Pacific spiny dogfish. The sharks were identified simply as lanternsharks. No photographs or specimens were retained. Voucher specimens for British Columbia are only a matter of time.

Order Squatiniformes (Angel sharks)

Worldwide, the angel sharks are all included in a single family and genus. This genus contains only 15 known species, one of which is present in BC waters. Angel sharks are bottom dwellers and have adapted to life on the ocean bottom to such an extent that they have a ray-like appearance, except that the pectoral fins are not attached to the head.

They have two dorsal fins and no anal fin, and unusually, the lower lobe of the caudal fin is longer than the upper lobe. There is one species of angel shark present in BC waters.

Family: Squatinidae (angel sharks)
Dorsoventrally flattened to resemble skates or rays; pectoral fins not attached to the head but cover the gill slits

Squatina californica (Pacific angel shark)
Teeth in both jaws are single, large, sharply pointed cusps; large pectoral fins clearly separated from the head; gills lateral and anterior to but covered or partially covered by the pectoral fins

Quick Bite

Bony fish have an air-filled swim bladder to control buoyancy, but sharks do not. Sharks use their large, oily livers as a kind of internal flotation device.

Pacific angel shark

Squatina californica
FAMILY Squatinidae (angel sharks)

CONSERVATION STATUS
Not Listed (Canada's Species at Risk Act)
Not Assessed (COSEWIC)
NT Near Threatened (IUCN Red List)

DESCRIPTION

The Pacific angel shark is distinctive in appearance, with a flattened body and large pectoral fins. The flattened body, along with the dorsal eyes, makes it easy to distinguish from other sharks. The large pectoral fins are clearly separated from the head, and the gill slits are partially on the sides of the head, making it easy to distinguish from skates and rays. The back ranges from greyish brown to reddish with speckled dark spots;

IMAGE 14 Pacific angel shark (*Squatina californica*)
The first record of this species in our waters
occurred quite recently, in 2016. PHOTO: A. MURCH.

the belly is white. The Pacific angel shark has a large mouth at the end of
its snout with barbels on the anterior margin. The teeth in both jaws are
similar, consisting of single, large, sharply pointed cusps.

RANGE

The Pacific angel shark is common in the eastern Pacific, particularly
off California and Mexico, and has been reported once (1903) as far
north as southeastern Alaska. The only record of a Pacific angel shark
in British Columbia was made in 2016 by a diver off Clover Point,
Victoria (southwest Vancouver Island). The shark was photographed in
approximately 12 m of water, resting motionless on the bottom. The diver
estimated the shark to be approximately 1.2 m long.

GENERAL BIOLOGY

Pacific angel sharks are thought to live up to 35 years. The maximum size is 1.2 m for males and 1.5 m for females. Both males and females mature at about 1.0 m length and about 10 years of age. Pacific angel sharks are viviparous, without a yolk-sac placenta, and give birth to litters of 1–13 young. Birth takes place in spring following a 10-month gestation period.

ECOLOGY

Pacific angel sharks are found in temperate waters on the continental shelf. They occupy depths of 3–183 m but are usually found at depths less than 100 m. It is a demersal (bottom-dwelling) shark, found on sandy or muddy flat bottoms close to reefs or kelp forests.

This species is an ambush predator, and remains motionless and partially covered by sand waiting to strike at passing prey. It feeds mainly on bony fishes and squid. Angel sharks are preyed upon by larger sharks including the broadnose sevengill shark and the great white shark.

USE

A commercial drift-net fishery for Pacific angel sharks operated in California out of Santa Barbara from the late 1970s through the 1980s until 1990, when fishing for this shark was banned. A commercial fishery for Pacific angel shark exists in Mexico, both along the Pacific coast and in the Gulf of California.

Quick Bite
Sharks have phenomenal hearing. They can hear prey from as far away as 900 metres. Their hearing is so good that they can hear sounds such as a struggling fish's contracting muscle.

Order Lamniformes (Mackerel sharks)

The mackerel sharks are a small and diverse group that contains some of the best-known sharks. They include some of the most famous species and feared hunters, such as the great white shark, mako shark, salmon shark, common thresher shark and basking shark.

Although the species in this group appear quite diverse, they have a number of common features such as a pointed snout, two dorsal fins (neither of which has a spine), an anal fin and five paired gill slits. All mackerel sharks lack a nictitating membrane to protect the eyes. The mouths of these sharks are large, with jaws that extend far back to allow them to open extremely wide to gulp down large prey or chunks of flesh. In the case of the basking shark, the large mouth allows them to filter large volumes of water and sieve plankton through bristle-like structures in their mouths.

As a whole, this group has a global distribution from sub-polar regions to the tropics. The mackerel sharks have a special adaptation of their circulatory system that allows them to retain heat from internal metabolic processes, which makes them warm-blooded. This allows them to spend more energy on swimming and hunting rather than on maintaining their body temperature as the surrounding water cools. This ability to withstand changing water temperatures makes them one of the most prolific, abundant and geographically widespread shark groups.

In BC waters we have five species representing this group.

Family: Lamnidae (mackerel sharks)
Large triangular, blade-like teeth

Carcharodon carcharias (great white shark)
Broad, serrated teeth; origin of first dorsal fin largely posterior to pectoral fin; white belly without blotches

Isurus oxyrinchus (shortfin mako shark)
Long, narrow teeth without serrations; origin of first dorsal fin largely posterior to pectoral fin; white belly without blotches

Lamna ditropis (salmon shark)
Long, narrow teeth without serrations; origin of first dorsal fin directly over the inner margin of pectoral fin; white belly with numerous dusky blotches

Family: Cetorhinidae (basking sharks)
Numerous minute hook-shaped teeth; extremely large gill slits extending onto the surface of the head; bristle-like gill rakers

Cetorhinus maximus (basking shark)
Large stout-bodied shark with a conical snout, large mouth and enormous gill slits; numerous minute teeth (about 100 per row) with a single cusp

Family: Alopiidae (thresher sharks)
Small numerous teeth; small gill slits; large curved caudal fin

Alopias vulpinus (common thresher shark)
Teeth are small and curved without cusplets; upper lobe of caudal fin as long as the body

Great white shark

Carcharodon carcharias
FAMILY Lamnidae (mackerel sharks)

CONSERVATION STATUS
Not Listed (Canada's Species at Risk Act)
Data Deficient (COSEWIC)
VU Vulnerable (IUCN Red List)

DESCRIPTION
Great white sharks have a distinctive deep-crescent-shaped caudal fin.
Another feature that helps to identify them is their large, triangular
and heavily serrated teeth. The teeth of the lower jaw are narrower,
protruding from the mouth even when closed. The body is a heavy
spindle shape, and the snout is bluntly conical. Despite their name, their
backs and sides are a uniform blue-grey to brown colour, with white
only on their bellies. Typically, there is a black spot on the body near the
base of the pectoral fin, and the pectoral fin tips are usually black. The
iris of the eye is conspicuously black. It is the only living species of the
genus *Carcharodon*.

IMAGE 15   Great white shark (*Carcharodon carcharias*)
Perhaps the world's most famous shark, it is a rare visitor
to BC waters. PHOTO: A. MURCH.

RANGE

The species is worldwide in distribution, but mainly in temperate
and subtropical oceans. In the Pacific they are found from the Gulf of
California up to the Gulf of Alaska. Off of British Columbia, in outer
coastal waters, there are only about a half dozen confirmed occurrences,
with numerous unconfirmed reports. The great white shark has been
recorded from Esperanza Inlet on the west coast of Vancouver Island and
from Hecate Strait from their strandings on the shores of the Haida Gwaii.

GENERAL BIOLOGY

The maximum age for great white sharks is estimated to be 60 years.
There is some disagreement as to their maximum size, though it is
known that they can exceed 7 m. The largest verified great white shark
from BC waters is a 5.2 m shark that was stranded on Graham Island,
Haida Gwaii. Males reach maturity at 8–10 years and a length of 3.5–4 m;
females reach maturity between 12 and 18 years at a length of 4–5 m.

The reproduction of the great white shark is ovoviviparous, meaning
the young hatch within the female's body before being released. The
gestation period is unknown. The reproductive cycle is also unknown,

but females may take more than 3 years between litters to rebuild their energy stores. Litter sizes vary from 2 to 10, and may be as high as 17. The length of pups at birth is estimated to be 1.1–1.7 m. Off the west coast of North America, the great white shark pupping area is probably in southern California.

ECOLOGY

They are generally found in shallow coastal waters, often near the surface, but great white sharks have been captured at depths of more than 1,200 m. Aside from being a famous movie star (*Jaws*), great whites are best known as man-eating sharks. The great white shark is a highly visual animal with a retina that is well adapted to acute and possibly full-colour vision. The great white shark will visually investigate objects such as boats and surfboards at the surface, and it is this behaviour that often brings this shark into contact with humans. In addition, their attacks on people are likely a result of their preference for marine mammals (seals, sea lions and sea otters) and turtles, which a swimming human could be mistaken for.

Besides marine mammals, great white sharks feed on large fish (such as other sharks) and smaller fishes such as Pacific salmon, Pacific hake and rockfishes. They are also scavengers, and have been observed feeding on floating cetacean carcasses. The only noted predators of great white sharks are offshore killer whales. There is some research that indicates that the great white shark exhibits social behaviours, and may travel in small but stable groups.

USE

It has been noted that great white sharks are suitable food fish. They are valued for their jaws, teeth and fins, and have been targeted by sport fisheries and commercial fisheries in some parts of the world. However, it is illegal to retain a great white shark in British Columbia, California, South Africa and various states of Australia.

Quick Bite
Since both humans and sharks are jawed vertebrates, we share a common ancestor. In fact, our genetic information that is associated with metabolism has similarity to the same genetic coding in great white sharks.

Very few shark species attack humans, and of the ones listed in this book, only the great white shark and shortfin mako shark are considered dangerous. Good thing these sharks are rare in BC waters.

IMAGE 16 **Shortfin mako shark** (*Isurus oxyrinchus*) A highly migratory species that is rarely found in our waters. PHOTO: A. MURCH.

Quick Bite

The shortfin mako shark is recognized as the fastest shark, with a record speed of 95 kilometres per hour. Keep that in mind next time you are driving on the highway!

Shortfin mako shark

Isurus oxyrinchus
FAMILY Lamnidae (mackerel sharks)

CONSERVATION STATUS
Not Listed (Canada's Species at Risk Act)
Not Assessed (COSEWIC)
VU Vulnerable (IUCN Red List)

DESCRIPTION

Shortfin mako sharks are easily identified by their long, pointed nose and large keel (raised area) on the caudal peduncle. Their bodies are streamlined, tapering to a narrow caudal peduncle. They are a deep blue colour on their backs, with white bellies. Their teeth are elongated and narrow without serrated edges.

RANGE

Worldwide in temperate and subtropical oceans. In the north Pacific they range from south of the Aleutian Islands to Baja California. There are numerous unconfirmed reports of shortfin mako sharks occurring off Haida Gwaii and Vancouver Island. The only confirmed specimens are one captured in 1992 off Cape St. James in Haida Gwaii and a second that washed ashore on the west coast of Vancouver Island in 2016.

Acoustic tagging studies indicate that shortfin mako sharks do occupy waters off northern Washington, so it is likely that they infrequently occupy BC waters.

GENERAL BIOLOGY

Their maximum size is 4 m. The maximum age has been estimated as 29 years for males and 32 years for females. There is, however, recent evidence to suggest that these ages may be overestimated by at least 10 years. Males mature at age 4 years, and females between 7 and 8 years. The size at maturity for males is 1.9 m and for females is 2.7–3.0 m.

Shortfin mako sharks are ovoviviparous, meaning the young hatch within the female's body before being released, and they show oophagous intrauterine cannibalism. They have a 3-year reproductive cycle, with a 15- to 18-month gestation period followed by a 15- to 18-month resting period. Pups are born from late winter to mid-spring. Litter sizes can be from 4 to 25 pups, and at birth pups are approximately 70 cm.

ECOLOGY

Shortfin mako sharks are a surface (epipelagic) species, but have been found at depths to 150 m. Their body and caudal peduncle shape, along with being warm-blooded, allow them to attain speeds of up to 95 km per hour, giving them the reputation of being the fastest-swimming shark.

This great speed allows shortfin mako sharks to outswim their prey so that they can capture fast swimmers such as mackerel and tuna, swordfish, common dolphinfish and other sharks. They also eat Pacific herring, anchovy and Pacific sardines as well as squid. Killer whales have been observed preying on shortfin mako sharks.

USE

Commercial longline and drift-net fisheries off Washington, Oregon and California have targeted this fish. Shortfin mako sharks are a popular sport fish in California, not only because they are exceptionally good to eat, but also because their agility and speed make them strong fighters. They are a popular and frequent menu item in North American restaurants.

Salmon shark

Lamna ditropis
FAMILY Lamnidae (mackerel sharks)

CONSERVATION STATUS
Not Listed (Canada's Species at Risk Act)
Not Assessed (COSEWIC)
LC Least Concern (IUCN Red List)

DESCRIPTION

The salmon shark has a narrow caudal peduncle with a well-defined keel (raised area). The salmon shark's most distinctive identifying characteristic is a second, small keel just behind the main one on the caudal peduncle. They come in all sorts of colours, ranging from grey or black to dark blue grey. The belly is white and can have dusky blotches and spots. It has a stubby snout and well-developed eyes. The teeth are large and similar in size in the upper and lower jaws. Each tooth has a smooth-edged cusp and smaller cusplets on each side. The salmon shark is often mistaken for the famous great white shark, since it looks like a smaller, huskier version.

RANGE

The salmon shark is found throughout the north Pacific in temperate and subarctic waters. They range from the Bering Sea, through the Gulf of Alaska and down to Mexico in the eastern Pacific and to Korea in the western Pacific. They are common throughout BC waters off the west coast of Vancouver Island and Haida Gwaii in Queen Charlotte Sound, Hecate Strait and Dixon Entrance.

GENERAL BIOLOGY

This shark is short and stout, with a maximum size of about 3 m. The maximum age of salmon sharks is estimated as between 17 years (females) and 25 years (males). Males mature in 5 years, and females in 9–10 years. Salmon sharks mate off Alaska in autumn. Salmon sharks are ovoviviparous, meaning the young hatch within the female's body before being released, and they show oophagous intrauterine cannibalism, with the late-stage embryos whose yolk sacs are depleted obtaining their nourishment by feeding on unfertilized eggs. The average litter size is 2–5 pups, born in late spring after a 12-month gestation. The pups are born at sizes between 65 and 85 cm.

ECOLOGY

Salmon sharks are a surface species, but have been found at depths to 375 m. They inhabit close, inshore waters out to deep, oceanic waters. They are one of the few sharks with a range that extends into very cold waters due to their ability to maintain a body temperature up to 16°C higher than the surrounding water. This warm-bloodedness, which is shared with the other mackerel sharks (family Lamnidae), enables the salmon shark to maintain fast swimming speeds with its warm swimming muscles, making it a formidable predator, able to outswim many of its prey.

These compact sharks are voracious feeders. As their name implies, their favourite prey is salmon; in fact, their flesh is often a salmon-red colour because of their preference for this food. Adult salmon sharks often follow schools of Pacific salmon, forming hunting aggregates of 30–40 sharks. When feeding on salmon, these sharks are tenacious and energetic, often leaping out of the water with a captured salmon. When

IMAGE 17 **Salmon shark** (*Lamna ditropis*)
This shark is often mistaken for a small great white shark. It is distinguishable from a great white shark by its elongated teeth and grey mottling on the white belly. PHOTO: A. MURCH.

not feeding on salmon, these sharks will prey on anything available. Other prey species recorded include walleye pollock, Pacific herring, lingcod, chub mackerel, Pacific tomcod, sculpins (family Cottidae), Pacific spiny dogfish and squid. Salmon sharks are eaten by killer whales.

USE
Salmon sharks are occasionally captured by recreational anglers, commercial longliners and gillnetters. A small experimental drift-gillnet fishery was conducted off Canada in the early 1990s, but a commercial fishery never materialized because of poor economics. A commercial fishery for salmon sharks occurs off Japan and in the central north Pacific. There is a recreational fishery for salmon sharks in Alaska, and because of this, and their highly migratory nature, they are unfortunately allowed to be retained by recreational fishers in British Columbia as well.

Quick Bite

Sharks are not the most dangerous animals in the world. While sharks kill an average of less than 1 person a year in the United States and 5 to 10 worldwide, hippos kill 2,900 people a year in Africa. Closer to home, deer are responsible for about 130 deaths a year, usually due to car collisions.

IMAGE 18

Basking shark caught by fishermen off central British Columbia in July 1901.
PHOTO: BC ARCHIVES D-02035.

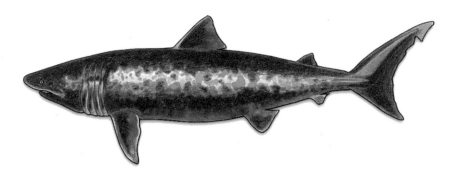

Basking shark

Cetorhinus maximus
FAMILY Cetorhinidae (basking sharks)

CONSERVATION STATUS

EN Endangered (Canada's Species at Risk Act)
EN Endangered (COSEWIC)
EN Endangered (IUCN Red List)

DESCRIPTION

The basking shark is one of the few sharks that is not a flesh eater. Along with the whale shark (*Rhincodon typus*) and the megamouth shark (*Megachasma pelagios*), the basking shark is a filter-feeder that uses modified gill rakers to capture plankton in the water. However, basking sharks still do possess numerous tiny teeth, each with a single backward-curving cusp. Since it uses its gill rakers to filter water, the gill slits are enormous in size, almost encircling the head. It is grey brown to grey black with a white belly. The basking shark is the only living member of the family Cetorhinidae.

RANGE

Basking sharks have a worldwide distribution in temperate and cold waters. In the Pacific they are found from Baja California to the Gulf of Alaska; from Peru to Ecuador; from Kamchatka to China; and around southern Australia and New Zealand. They were common in the early to mid-20th century throughout BC waters, including inner coastal waters such as the Strait of Georgia and inlets on the west coast of Vancouver Island; however, following the eradication program of the 1960s, they are now rare and may only be limited to the west coast of Vancouver Island. At present, basking sharks appear infrequently in BC waters with only 33 confirmed sightings since 1996, 3 of which were incidentally captured in fisheries.

GENERAL BIOLOGY

Very little research has been conducted on basking sharks in the Pacific. Much of the information on the general biology (and ecology) comes from research conducted on Atlantic populations. Basking sharks are rarely encountered until they have reached 3 m in length, so information on early life history is particularly sparse. Basking sharks live approximately 50 years, with males maturing between 12 and 16 years and females between 16 and 20 years. Basking sharks are the second-largest shark in the world (whale sharks are the largest) reaching lengths of 10 m. Length of maturity for males is estimated to be between 4.5 to 6 m, and is unknown for females.

The life cycle of basking sharks is poorly understood but is probably similar to other mackerel sharks. Mating is thought to occur in early summer based on observed courtship behaviour and scarring. Nose-to-tail circling at the surface is thought to be associated with courtship and mating. Observations of pregnant females for this species are based on a single record of a shark with a litter of 6 young estimated to be 1.5–2 m, which is likely close to their size at birth. The basking shark is thought to be ovoviviparous, meaning the young hatch within the female's body before being released, and oophagous, referring to intrauterine cannibalism. Gestation has been estimated (not verified) to be 2.6 years assuming a size at birth of 1.5 m. Time between litters has been estimated at 2–4 years.

The basking shark periodically shed their gill rakers, which has given rise to theories about how they maintain their energetic requirements while not feeding. One possibility is that their massive livers, which make up to 25 per cent of the body weight, may act as an energy store while the gill rakers regenerate.

IMAGE 19 **Basking shark** (*Cetorhinus maximus*)
The second-largest fish in the world. This gentle
giant feeds exclusively on plankton. PHOTO: A. MURCH.

ECOLOGY

Information on the habitat range of basking sharks is incomplete.
As their name implies, on calm days they congregate at the surface,
presumably to feed. It is known that they often swim just below the
surface. To filter out plankton (copepods, larvae and fish eggs), the
basking shark cruises through the water with its mouth wide open
and its gill slits distended, filtering about 2,000 litres of water an hour.
Since basking sharks are born close to 1.5–2 m long, they have very few
predators. Other sharks, such as great white sharks, and killer whales
may be potential predators, but there has never been a substantiated kill
by either species. The lack of natural predators suggests that humans are
likely the largest source of mortality.

In the northeast Pacific, basking sharks were most visibly abundant
in spring and summer off British Columbia and Washington, and off
California in autumn and winter. Based on these observations, it has
been inferred that the northeast Pacific population may undergo a
seasonal migration. Similarly, off the Atlantic seaboard, their seasonal
appearances moving from south to north between spring and summer
have been used to support the theory of an annual latitudinal migration.

Basking sharks historically were sighted as large aggregations. Off British Columbia's coast, there are several bays and small inlets, such as Pachena Bay or Alberni Inlet, that have anecdotal and/or newspaper accounts of noteworthy high densities of sharks. Aggregations in Clayoquot Sound were observed up until the mid-1990s.

USE

From 1900 to 1970, basking sharks were subject to a commercial harvest, a directed eradication program, incidental catch and sport harpooning. In the first part of the 20th century, oil from their large livers was used as fuel in lamps. Based on economic data and newspaper sources, it appears that the war-era commercial fishery for basking shark liver was likely limited to the years between 1941 and 1947. Unfortunately, all basking shark landings were lumped together and reported as "Mixed Shark," which comprised brown catshark, blue shark, Pacific sleeper shark, salmon shark and basking shark. Fisheries statistics from this era make no reference to basking shark landings, as the products of the basking sharks were likely sold and categorized as reduction products such as fish oils, fish meal or fish fertilizer.

In British Columbia, during the mid-1940s until the late 1960s, basking sharks were seen as a nuisance species because they were numerous in certain areas and became entangled in fishing nets. The outcry from commercial fishers was so great that fishery patrol boats were outfitted with underwater knives and eradicated hundreds of basking sharks. Other eradication methods were also used including shooting and harpooning by patrol vessels, opportunistically ramming basking sharks with both patrol and commercial vessels, and sport fishing using harpoons. Since the eradication program, basking sharks rarely occur in BC waters.

Quick Bite

Basking sharks, the gentle giants of the sea, are the second-largest fish in the world, measuring up to 10 metres. Have no fear—these filter-feeding sharks only consume tiny plankton. Basking sharks suck in the equivalent of 10,000 large bottles of plankton-filled seawater in one hour.

Illustration (left) and photo of the bow-mounted sharp blade used on ships off Vancouver Island for the eradication of basking sharks in the 1950s and 1960s.

PHOTOS: REPRODUCED WITH PERMISSION, *POPULAR MECHANICS*, 1956.

IMAGE 21

Basking sharks are listed as Endangered in Pacific Canada. Sightings of this once common shark are now rare. Fisheries and Oceans Canada runs a website that invites the public to record occurrences as part of monitoring population recovery (pac.dfo-mpo.gc.ca/SharkSightings). Sightings are limited to times when a shark is at the surface. Visible is the tall, triangular dorsal fin with the bulbous snout protruding as the shark opens its large mouth to filter-feed. PHOTO: T. NORGARD.

Common thresher shark

Alopias vulpinus
FAMILY Alopiidae (thresher sharks)

CONSERVATION STATUS
Not Listed (Canada's Species at Risk Act)
Not Assessed (COSEWIC)
 Vulnerable (IUCN Red List)

DESCRIPTION

The common thresher shark is easy to recognize because it has an extremely long upper lobe of the caudal fin. This lobe is about half the length of the whole body and, with its curvature, resembles a scythe. They are complexly coloured: their backs can be purple, grey, brown, blue or black; their sides can be silvery, blue or golden; and their bellies are white but can have dark patches. The snout is short and conical. The teeth are relatively small with a single smooth, slightly curved, triangular cusp.

RANGE

The common thresher shark is found globally in warm temperate waters. In the north Pacific, it is found around Hawaii, off California, in the Gulf of California and around Japan and Taiwan. The common thresher shark exhibits strong seasonal migrations following warm water. It is abundant off Vancouver Island in summer and early fall. It has also been confirmed in commercial catches from Hecate Strait and the west coast of Haida Gwaii.

GENERAL BIOLOGY

They can grow to lengths of 5.7 m, but most are about 4–5 m. Maximum age is 15 years. Males mature at a size of about 3.3 m, corresponding to an age of about 3–7 years. Females mature at a larger size of 4.2 m, but there are no current estimates for age of maturity.

They are oophagous, since developing embryos will eat eggs in the uterus. Mating occurs in late summer, July to August. The common thresher shark has one of the shortest gestation periods, at 9 months, after which birth occurs the following spring, between March and June. Females give birth to litter sizes of 2–4 pups, which are each about 1.2–1.5 m long.

ECOLOGY

Common thresher sharks are found in coastal waters, but they sometimes venture far from shore. They inhabit waters from the surface down to depths of 350 m.

The common thresher shark eats squid and small fish, such as the Pacific herring, anchovy and Pacific sardine. It is reported that these sharks actually use their large tails to herd their prey and then kill them with long, sweeping strikes. There is debate on the validity of these speculations, particularly about the ability of the tail to kill or stun prey. However, such a dramatic biological feature must provide some function, and it is generally accepted that it is used to herd schooling fishes. It is also probable that this tail provides additional propulsion power for swimming.

USE

Worldwide, there is a market for fresh, frozen, smoked and dried thresher meat. Its liver is processed for vitamins, its skin is used as a leather and its fins are used in shark fin soup. International commercial fisheries for common thresher use gillnet and longline gear to capture them. They are also a popular sport fish off southern California. In British Columbia they are infrequently captured in commercial fisheries.

Order Carcharhiniformes (Ground sharks)

The ground sharks are the most dominant, diverse shark group with over 270 different species worldwide. They are found in almost every marine environment from cold to tropical waters and shallow coastal to deep ocean waters. Some species are known to enter freshwater river systems. This order contains some of the smallest and some of the largest-known shark species. Some ground shark species exhibit very specialized body forms, such as the laterally flattened head of the hammerhead shark.

Most ground sharks have two dorsal fins (no spines), an anal fin, five pairs of gill slits and a lower nictitating membrane to protect the eyes. Members of this group have a particularly long snout, and a long mouth extending behind the eyes.

This order is represented by four species in BC waters.

Family: Scyliorhinidae (catsharks)

Both dorsal fins are small, with first dorsal fin directly above the pelvic fin; anal fin larger than either dorsal fin; teeth small and cuspidate (has cusps)

Apristurus brunneus (brown catshark)

Teeth similar in both jaws, with large central cusp and one or two small cusps on each side; body small, slender and flabby; snout and head long and laterally extended

Family: Triakidae (houndsharks)

First dorsal fin is large and anterior to pelvic fin; anal fin similar in size to small second dorsal fin; broad teeth, with small cusplets on either side of each tooth

Galeorhinus galeus (tope (soupfin) shark)

Teeth blade-like and compressed with one large smooth cusp followed by four or five smaller cusplets; snout long and pointed; second dorsal fin much smaller than the first

Family: Carcharhinidae (requiem sharks)

Large, fusiform-shaped bodies; eyes round with nictitating membranes; first dorsal fin much larger than second; teeth blade-like

Prionace glauca (blue shark)

Triangular upper teeth with curved cusps having serrated edges; triangular, straight lower teeth with finely serrated cusps; long pointed snout; pectoral fin long and sabre-like

Family: Sphyrnidae (hammerhead sharks)

Head laterally expanded into a hammer shape

Sphyrna zygaena (smooth hammerhead shark)

Triangular teeth have a single oblique cusp; upper teeth larger than lower; large hammer-shaped head with a smooth margin

Brown catshark

Apristurus brunneus
FAMILY Scyliorhinidae (catsharks)

CONSERVATION STATUS
Not Listed (Canada's Species at Risk Act)
Data Deficient (COSEWIC)
Data Deficient (IUCN Red List)

DESCRIPTION
Distinguishing characteristics of the brown catshark include their coloration and the shape of their eyes. The brown catshark is a uniform dark brown with lightly coloured fin edges. Their eyes are elongated and deeply set. Brown catsharks have nictitating membranes (eyelids), a feature limited to a few families of sharks. Their head and snout are long and flattened. Teeth are small, with a large central cusp and one or two small cusplets on each side. For BC sharks, size is a distinguishing characteristic, since they are the smallest shark inhabiting our waters.

RANGE
The brown catshark is found throughout the eastern Pacific Ocean from southern Alaska through to southern California, including into the Gulf of California and down Central and South America off Panama, Ecuador, Peru and Chile. In British Columbia, it is very common in deep slope and coastal shelf areas.

GENERAL BIOLOGY
The brown catshark is small. Its maximum size is only 70 cm, and most are about 40–50 cm. Maximum age and age at maturity for this species

are unknown. Size at maturity is currently estimated to be about 50 cm for both males and females. Brown catsharks are the only sharks in BC waters that are oviparous, laying egg cases with one developing embryo inside. Two egg cases are extruded at the same time, one from each oviduct, and the gestation time in the oviduct is quite short. The egg cases are translucent and oblong, about 5 cm long, with long tendrils for attachment to the bottom. Egg cases are deposited year-round in areas of high vertical relief at depths between 300 and 400 m. The incubation period in the egg cases may be as long as 27 months. Embryos hatch at a length of 7–9 cm.

ECOLOGY
Adult brown catsharks eat shrimp (family Pandalidae), krill (family Euphausiidae), small squid and small bony fishes. Egg cases are preyed upon by predatory snails. Off British Columbia, adults are thought to be eaten by other, larger elasmobranchs. The brown catshark inhabits coastal shelf regions and deepwater slope areas down to 1,300 m.

USE
There is no commercial use of brown catsharks. In British Columbia they are a common bycatch in trawl fisheries.

IMAGE 22   **Brown catshark** (*Apristurus brunneus*)
This is the smallest shark found in BC waters, generally less than half a metre long. PHOTO: A. MURCH.

Tope (soupfin) shark

Galeorhinus galeus
FAMILY Triakidae (houndsharks)

CONSERVATION STATUS
SC Special Concern (Canada's Species at Risk Act)
SC Special Concern (COSEWIC)
VU Vulnerable (IUCN Red List)

DESCRIPTION

The most distinguishing feature of the tope shark is the large, sharply defined terminal lobe of the caudal fin. They are a dark-bluish to grey colour on their backs fading to a white belly. Their snouts are elongated and pointed. The teeth are small, triangular and blade-like, with a single smooth-edged cusp followed by a number of smaller cusplets. Their maximum size is 2.5 m, though most are only 1.5–2 m long. Previously, these sharks were identified as *Galeorhinus zyopterus*. It is also commonly known as the soupfin shark.

RANGE

Worldwide but discontinuous distribution in some cold and warm temperate waters. They are not found in the western north Pacific nor the western north Atlantic. In the eastern Pacific, they range from British Columbia to the Gulf of California, and are also found off Peru, Chile and Argentina. In BC waters they are common along the west coast of Vancouver Island, and in Queen Charlotte Sound and Hecate Strait.

Shark skin feels like sandpaper because it is made up of tiny teeth-like structures called placoid scales, also known as denticles. Coastal First Nations used the Pacific spiny dogfish skin as sandpaper for any woodworking needs.

GENERAL BIOLOGY

Tope sharks in the northeast Pacific reach maximum lengths of 2 m for females and 1.8 m for males. Age estimates for tope sharks in British Columbia are not available; however, based on a tagged shark in Australia that was at liberty for 35 years, the estimated maximum age for this species is 45 years. In the northeast Pacific, females are mature at a total length of 1.5 m and males are mature at 1.3 m. Elsewhere, the ages of maturity are estimated to be about 13–15 years for females and 12–17 years for males.

Little is known about the breeding behaviour of tope sharks. However, observations of females with unfertilized eggs in May suggest that fertilization occurs soon after, by late spring. Tope sharks are ovoviviparous, meaning the young hatch within the female's body before being released, with females carrying 6–52 pups. Globally, the gestation period is thought to be 12 months. Parturition (the process of giving birth) is thought to occur between March and July, with pups being an average of 35–37 cm long.

ECOLOGY

Tope sharks are a coastal pelagic species, often associated with bottom habitat. They are found in temperate continental-shelf waters from close inshore, including shallow bays, to well offshore, but not high seas. They range from the surface down to depths of 470 m, and are often associated with canyons. Pups and juveniles use shallow nearshore habitats for 1–2 years before moving offshore.

Limited tagging study results from California and British Columbia suggest that some tope sharks undergo extended migrations between the two areas, and that they are capable of travelling long distances in a short time. The tope shark is indeed a highly mobile shark, travelling up to 55 km per day. In some studies, they have been recorded moving up to 1,500 km away from the initial capture site. Additionally, there appear to be both movements in depth and across latitudes that vary by both sex and season. For example, female tope sharks are present in southern California in shallow waters during spring, and males are present in northern California in deep waters during fall.

The tope shark is opportunistic, feeding on schooling fishes such as Pacific herring, Pacific sardine, anchovy, smelt (family Osmeridae) and Pacific hake, as well as bottom fish such as Pacific cod, rockfish, flatfish and sablefish. They will also feed on cephalopods such as squid and octopus and an assortment of other bottom invertebrates, such as crab and shrimp. They also feed on other sharks, skates and rays. Tope sharks are eaten by other elasmobranchs including the great white shark and the

IMAGE 23 **Tope shark** (*Galeorhinus galeus*) This shark is being released after sampling and satellite tagging off the west coast of Vancouver Island. The tope shark is also commonly known as the soupfin shark, based on its historic commercial use for shark fin soup. PHOTO: J. KING.

broadnose sevengill shark and possibly by marine mammals such as the killer whale.

USE

Part of the reason that tope shark was originally called the soupfin shark is the extensive fisheries in the 1930s and 1940s where the fins were dried, exported to Asia and used in soup. As with many other shark species, the liver of the tope shark has been used as a source of vitamin A. The liver of this species contains the highest concentration of vitamin A of any fish on the Pacific coast, which made them the most valuable shark.

Tope sharks were the target of a brief but extensive commercial liver fishery throughout their northeast Pacific range beginning in 1937 in California and continuing in British Columbia, Oregon and Washington in the early 1940s. The Canadian fishery took place primarily off the west coast of Vancouver Island and in Hecate Strait with a variety of fishing gear including halibut longlines, dogfish longlines, trawls, sunken gillnets and drift nets. The BC fishery peaked in 1944 at approximately 278 tonnes. Canadian fishing magazines reported a decrease in Canadian abundance starting in 1944, and by 1946 the Canadian fishery had substantially diminished. The large fisheries in California (1938–1945) took over 10,000 tonnes and decimated the population, particularly in the nursery areas in San Francisco and Tomales Bays. Finally, in 1947 vitamin A was synthesized in a laboratory, which removed the demand for wild-caught sources.

The tope shark is now considered endangered because of intensive fisheries in some parts of the world, but commercial fisheries still target this species. It has become a popular sport fish in Britain, South Africa and California. They are still caught incidentally in commercial fisheries off British Columbia.

Quick Bite

The jaws of large sharks are about twice as powerful as the jaws of a lion, and can generate up to 40,000 psi of pressure in a single bite.

Blue shark

Prionace glauca
FAMILY Carcharhinidae (requiem sharks)

CONSERVATION STATUS
Not Listed (Canada's Species at Risk Act)
Not at Risk (COSEWIC)
Near Threatened (IUCN Red List)

DESCRIPTION
As the name implies, this shark has distinctive coloration with dark blue on the back, bright blue on the side, and a white belly. The blue shark has a sleek, streamlined body, with a long, pointed snout and very long, narrow pectoral fins. The upper teeth are triangular, curved and serrated on both edges, and the lower teeth are more erect triangular cusps that are smooth or finely serrated.

RANGE
Blue sharks have a global distribution, but the north Pacific stock is thought to be distinct from the south Pacific population. In the north Pacific, blue sharks range from the Gulf of Alaska down to the equator, where they are found at lower densities. In British Columbia they are

IMAGE 24 Blue shark (*Prionace glauca*)
This highly migratory shark travels
throughout the north Pacific, visiting our
waters in summer. PHOTO: A. MURCH.

common during summer months off the west coasts of Vancouver Island
and Haida Gwaii and in Queen Charlotte Sound and Hecate Strait.

GENERAL BIOLOGY

Blue sharks are often 2.5–3 m, with a maximum recorded size of 3.8 m.
The maximum age for blue sharks is estimated to be between 16 and 20
years. Females are considered to mature at sizes between 1.8 and 2.1 m
and ages 5–6 years. The males mature at approximately 2 m and younger
ages (4–6 years).

Blue shark reproduction is viviparous. Mating likely occurs in March
to August. Female blue sharks have thick skin on their backs, about two
to three times as thick as the skin of the male shark. Presumably, this is
to withstand the bites from males during mating. Observed litter sizes

in the Pacific range from 1 to 62 pups, with an average of about 25 pups; gestation is estimated to be between 9 and 12 months. Pups are born at lengths typically between 40 and 50 cm, although a range between 35 and 60 cm has been reported in the literature.

ECOLOGY

Blue sharks are essentially pelagic, normally occupying surface waters, but have been caught down to depths of 150 m. Blue sharks are fast swimming and highly migratory, with seasonal distributions corresponding to prey availability and their reproductive cycle. Mating occurs in the central north Pacific between latitude 20° and 30° north from about longitude 140° east, across the dateline, to 140° west. Pups are born at north of the mating area, between latitude 35° and 45° north. In summer, blue sharks migrate into coastal BC waters to feed. Blue sharks tagged off Vancouver Island moved extensively throughout the central and eastern north Pacific. Juvenile blue sharks segregate by sex: juvenile females occupy the pupping grounds and the region just to the north and into the Gulf of Alaska, whereas juvenile males occupy the pupping grounds but also the region just to the south.

The blue shark is most active at night, when it feeds mainly on squid and on small pelagic fish such as Pacific herring, Pacific sardine, chub mackerel, Pacific salmon and Pacific hake. They have also been known to eat some bottom fish, such as rockfish and flatfish, and some bottom invertebrates. They do eat other sharks, such as Pacific spiny dogfish and smaller blue sharks. Interestingly, blue sharks have gill rakers, which allow them to filter small organisms such as krill from the water column when other prey are scarce. Blue sharks do not actively hunt marine mammals but have been observed feeding on their carcasses. Sub-adults and juveniles are eaten by both shortfin mako sharks and great white sharks. In addition, California sea lions are reported to eat smaller blue sharks. There are no known predators of adult blue sharks.

USE

Blue sharks are the most heavily fished shark species in the world, and therefore humans have the greatest predatory impact on adult blue sharks. The blue shark is apparently good for smoking or drying, but the flesh takes on an ammonia taste soon after death, so it is not a popular food species. This shark is considered a sport fish in certain areas of the world; however, they cannot be retained in BC waters. They are considered to be a dangerous shark; there are numerous reports of attacks on humans. A number of divers have been harassed by blue sharks; however, it usually follows initial harassment by the divers.

Quick Bite
Internationally, there are approximately 75 species of shark on the endangered list.

Smooth hammerhead shark

Sphyrna zygaena
FAMILY Sphyrnidae (hammerhead sharks)

CONSERVATION STATUS
Not Listed (Canada's Species at Risk Act)
Not Assessed (COSEWIC)
VU Vulnerable (IUCN Red List)

DESCRIPTION

Hammerhead sharks are named after their distinctive, uniquely shaped head. The head is flattened and extends sideways, ending with an eye on each side. The head is called a cephalofoil, and many functions have been proposed for it including sensory reception and prey manipulation. The smooth hammerhead shark has a relatively small mouth. The triangular teeth have a single relatively smooth, oblique cusp, and the teeth in the upper jaw are slightly larger than those of the lower jaw. The smooth hammerhead lacks an indentation in the middle of the front edge of the

IMAGE 25   Smooth hammerhead shark (*Sphyrna zygaena*)
This species is easily distinguished by its hammer-shaped
head. It has been observed off of Vancouver Island only
twice, during the 1950s. PHOTO: A. MURCH.

head, giving it a smooth appearance. The smooth hammerhead has a
dark-olive to brownish-grey back, with a white belly.

RANGE

The smooth hammerhead shark is found in temperate waters from
central California to Baja California and down through the Gulf
of California. The only records of smooth hammerhead sharks
in BC waters are of two sharks captured by sport fishers near the
head of Barkley Sound (on the west coast of Vancouver Island) in
1953. These sharks were identified by museum curatorial staff.

GENERAL BIOLOGY

The maximum reported size for a smooth hammerhead is 4 m. Males
mature at a size of 2.5 m, females at 2.6 m.

They are viviparous, with a yolk-sac placenta. The gestation period is approximately 10–11 months, and the young are born in late spring to early summer. Litter sizes range from 20 to 50 pups, and young are 50–60 cm at birth.

ECOLOGY

They are the most cool-water-tolerant hammerhead species. The smooth hammerhead is a large, actively swimming shark found in nearshore waters out to the edge of the continental shelf. They generally swim in waters from near the surface to depths of 20 m.

Smooth hammerhead sharks can be found swimming in large schools during the day, but at night disperse for solitary hunting. They feed on cephalopods (octopus and squid), bony fish and smaller sharks, skates and rays.

USE

There are currently no commercial or recreational fisheries for smooth hammerheads in BC or US waters.

Quick Bite

We shouldn't be afraid of sharks; they should be afraid of us. Humans kill over 100 million sharks per year for their fins (for shark fin soup) and meat.

Skates and Rays

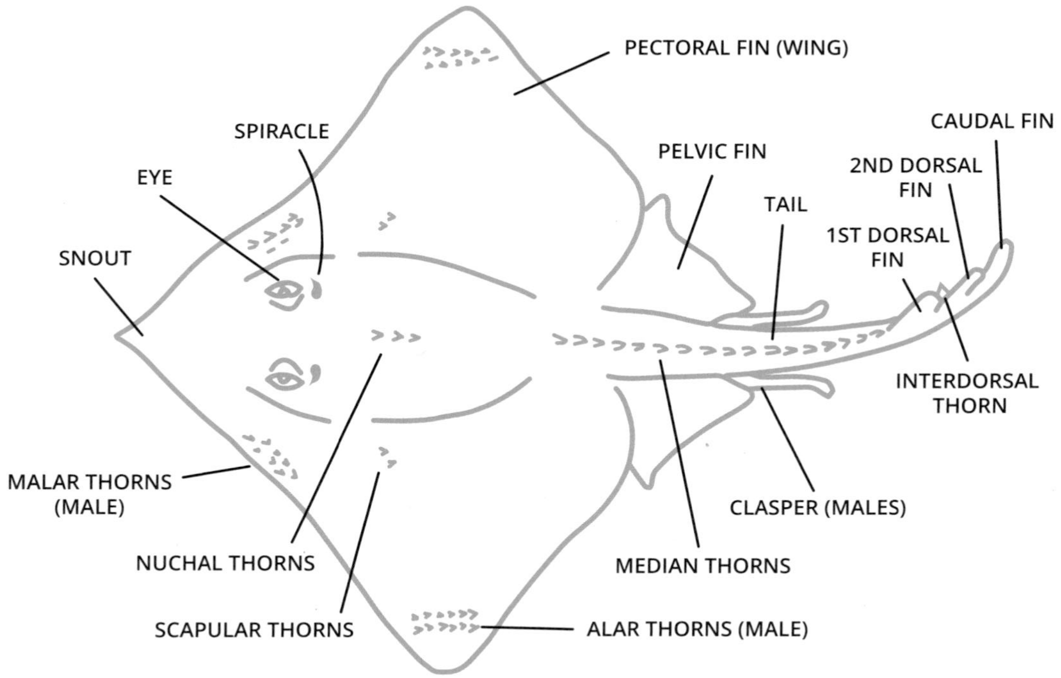

DIAGRAM 3

Morphological terminology of skates and rays used in this handbook.

(Note: Rays have a slightly different morphology than in the illustration.)

Labels on diagram:
- SNOUT
- EYE
- SPIRACLE
- MALAR THORNS (MALE)
- NUCHAL THORNS
- SCAPULAR THORNS
- PECTORAL FIN (WING)
- PELVIC FIN
- TAIL
- 2ND DORSAL FIN
- 1ST DORSAL FIN
- CAUDAL FIN
- INTERDORSAL THORN
- CLASPER (MALES)
- MEDIAN THORNS
- ALAR THORNS (MALE)

Order Rajiformes (Skates and rays)

Skates and rays have received far less attention than their "true shark" relatives, despite being the largest order of elasmobranchs. Currently, there are at least 600 species worldwide, a number continually increasing as more species are recognized. The Rajiformes include skates, stingrays, electric rays, sawfishes and guitarfishes (sawfishes and guitarfishes are not present in BC waters).

Skates and rays share a number of characteristics. They are defined largely by their adaptation to life on the ocean bottom (although not all are bottom dwellers). All are flattened, with the pectoral fins joined to the head and trunk to form a disc. The eyes and spiracles (the spiracles are a small respiratory opening) are on the upper (dorsal) side of the head, while the mouth and gill slits are on the lower (ventral) side.

Skates are characterized by a slender tail, usually with one or more rows of thorns or thornlets, but no stinging spine. They also have two small dorsal fins and a small caudal fin that may be absent in some species. Adults of many species show marked sexual dimorphism, with the disc outline of males becoming "bell shaped" compared to the females. In addition, males of many species develop specialized thorns on the dorsal surface of the wings (alar and malar thorns) that are used to hold the female skate during copulation.

Skates do not vary much in their body shape but can be separated by size, shape and colour as well as the presence or absence and distribution pattern of thorns. However, some species can be difficult to identify based on body measurements. This is especially true of the genus *Bathyraja*, where many of the species are a similar size and shape, which has led to problems with species identification. We touch on these problems as they apply to species within British Columbia within the individual species descriptions.

Electric rays have a short snout and a smooth dorsal surface without thorns or prickles. They possess kidney-shaped electric organs on the disc that can deliver a shock for defence or for subduing prey. Stingrays possess a whip-like tail with a large stinging spine.

The order Rajiformes is represented by 15 skate, 1 electric ray and 1 stingray species in BC waters.

Family: Arhynchobatidae (softnose skates)

Snout flabby and flexible; caudal fin small or absent; scattered denticles or prickles on the dorsal surface; most species have rows of thorns on the dorsal surface of the disc and tail

Bathyraja abyssicola (deepsea skate)

Snout flexible, long and narrow; no scapular thorns; disc with one to five nuchal thorns; prominent row of median thorns from pelvic region to first dorsal fin

Bathyraja aleutica (Aleutian skate)

Snout flexible and long; one or two prominent scapular thorns; continuous row of median thorns from head to first dorsal fin

Bathyraja kincaidii (sandpaper skate)

Snout flexible and short; prominent scapular thorns; interrupted or non-continuous row of median thorns from the mid-back to the first dorsal fin; dorsal surface of the disc covered with small sandpaper-like prickles

Bathyraja microtrachys (fine-spined skate)

Soft, triangular flexible snout; no scapular, nuchal or median thorns on the head; tail has a single row of well-developed thorns

Bathyraja interrupta (Bering skate)
Snout flexible with a triangular and rounded tip; prominent scapular and nuchal thorns, and an interrupted or non-continuous row of median thorns from the mid-back to the first dorsal fin; dorsal surface of the disc covered with small sandpaper-like prickles

Bathyraja trachura (roughtail skate)
Snout flexible and short; no scapular or nuchal thorns; prominent row of median thorns from the pelvic region to the first dorsal fin; dorsal surface covered with prominent prickles

Bathyraja parmifera (Alaska skate)
Snout flexible and short; prominent scapular and nuchal thorns; prominent median thorns from the head to the first dorsal fin with numerous prickles along each side of this row of thorns; margins of the wings covered with coarse denticles from the snout to the pelvic fin insertion

Bathyraja lindbergi (commander skate)
Snout flexible, short and broad; no scapular or nuchal thorns; well-developed median thorns from the head to the first dorsal fin; strongly developed thorns on the tail

Bathyraja minispinosa (whitebrow skate)
Snout flexible, long and pointed; no scapular thorns; nuchal thorns when present are small and few; prominent median thorns along the tail

Bathyraja spinosissima (Pacific white skate)
Snout flexible and short; no scapular or nuchal thorns; single row of median thorns on tail; dorsal and ventral surface of disc covered with small prickles

Family: Rajidae (hardnose skates)
Snout rigid and stiff; as with softnose skates, scattered denticles and thorns on the dorsal surface of the disc and tail

Amblyraja badia (broad skate)
Snout stiff and short with several thornlets on tip; triangular pattern of two to three scapular thorns; row of median thorns from the head to the tip of the tail, with the thorns on the tail flanked by numerous thornlets

Beringraja binoculata (previously *Raja binoculata*) (big skate)
Snout stiff and moderately pointed; dorsal surface covered with small prickles; no scapular thorns; one nuchal thorn; continuous row of median thorns from the pelvic region to the first dorsal fin

Raja rhina (longnose skate)
Snout stiff and extremely long, tapering to a point; dorsal surface with prickles; no scapular thorns; one or two nuchal thorns; continuous row of median thorns on the tail only

Raja stellulata (starry skate)
Snout stiff and short; dorsal surface covered with numerous star-shaped prickles; continuous, multiple rows of median thorns from the mid-back to the first dorsal fin

Raja inornata (California skate)
Snout stiff and long; no scapular thorns, but nuchal thorns present; median thorns from the mid-back to the first dorsal fin

Family: Torpedinidae (torpedo (electric) rays)
Short truncated snout; rounded disc with two moderately large dorsal fins; caudal fin prominent; skin smooth; two electric organs present

Tetronarce californica (also known as *Torpedo californica*) (Pacific torpedo (electric) ray)
Soft-bodied ray with an oval disc; small teeth with a single cusp; visible kidney-shaped electric organ; first dorsal fin much larger than the second

Family: Dasyatidae (whiptail stingrays)
Caudal fin absent; long whip-like tail with a large stinging spine

Pteroplatytrygon violacea (previously *Dasyatis violacea*) (pelagic stingray)
Broad wedge-shaped disc with a broadly rounded anterior margin and snout; extremely long stinging spine on the tail

Quick Bite

Stingray venom can also be used as an anaesthetic. In ancient Greece, dentists and doctors extracted the venom from stingray spines and injected it into their patients to numb the area before an operation. Who knew?

Deepsea skate

Bathyraja abyssicola
FAMILY Arhynchobatidae (softnose skates)

CONSERVATION STATUS
Not Listed (Canada's Species at Risk Act)
Not Assessed (COSEWIC)
Data Deficient (IUCN Red List)

DESCRIPTION
This skate is dark grey to dark brown or black. The ventral surface is actually darker than the dorsal, with whitish coloration around the mouth. This is unusual, since most skates have a similar or lighter ventral surface compared to the dorsal. The deepsea skate has a flexible snout, which together with the head makes a triangular disc margin. Deepsea skates have no scapular thorns, and only one to five nuchal thorns. There is a continuous row of median thorns along the tail, starting at the pelvic

region. Two dorsal fins, usually with an interdorsal thorn, and a small caudal fin are present.

RANGE

Deepsea skates are found from the Bering Sea down to Baja California in the eastern north Pacific and down to Japan in the western north Pacific. Off British Columbia they are found in deeper waters along the continental slope from southern Vancouver Island to northern Haida Gwaii.

GENERAL BIOLOGY

Deepsea skates can reach a maximum total length of 1.6 m. There are no age estimates for this species, so it is unknown how long they live, or at what ages males and females mature. It is known that males mature at sizes between 1.1 and 1.2 m, but there is no information on the size of maturity for females.

Deepsea skates are oviparous and deposit egg cases on the sea floor. Since these skates inhabit deep waters, knowledge of egg cases, embryos and newly hatched skates is lacking. The smallest free-swimming deepsea skate recorded is 34 cm in total length.

ECOLOGY

As the name implies, this species occupies deep waters, from 350 to 2,900 m, and is most commonly found at depths greater than 1,000 m. This habitat preference makes encounters with deepsea skates rare so that very little is known about them. Limited diet data indicate that the deepsea skate feeds on annelid worms, cephalopods, crabs, shrimp and bony fishes. Predators have yet to be identified.

USE

Deepsea skates are rarely captured in fisheries, and as such there is currently no market for this species. However, there are existing deep-sea trawl fisheries targeting species such as thornyhead rockfishes (*Sebastolobus* spp.), which periodically encounter deepsea skate.

Aleutian skate

Bathyraja aleutica
FAMILY Arhynchobatidae (softnose skates)

CONSERVATION STATUS
Not Listed (Canada's Species at Risk Act)
Not Assessed (COSEWIC)
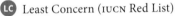
LC Least Concern (IUCN Red List)

DESCRIPTION
Aleutian skates have a grey to dark-brown dorsal surface, sometimes with black spots. The ventral surface is white with grey margins. The snout is flexible, broad and long, making up about two-thirds of the length of the head. This species has one to two strong, distinct scapular thorns. There is a single continuous row of prominent median thorns from the head to the first dorsal fin. Usually one or two interdorsal thorns are present. Aleutian skates have no caudal fin.

RANGE

Aleutian skates are found throughout the north Pacific along the outer continental shelf from northern California up to the Bering Sea and over to northern Japan. In BC waters, they are encountered along the continental slope off the west coasts of Vancouver Island and Haida Gwaii, as well as in Queen Charlotte Sound and Dixon Entrance.

GENERAL BIOLOGY

The maximum recorded total length for the Aleutian skate is 155 cm, and they live to a maximum age of 19 years. Males mature at about 113 cm, corresponding to 8–9 years old, and females mature at 125 cm, corresponding to 9–14 years.

Aleutian skates are oviparous and deposit egg cases with a single embryo. Their egg cases are covered in prickles and have one long horn at each of the four corners. Egg cases are very large, measuring from 12 cm to 14 cm long. Egg cases are deposited continuously between June and November, at depths between 250 and 500 m. Nursery grounds in British Columbia are unknown; however, those in the Bering Sea have been located near shelf breaks. The incubation period is unknown. Size at hatching is 12–15 cm.

ECOLOGY

Aleutian skates are commonly found at depths between 100 and 800 m, but can occur at depths to 1,500 m. Nothing is known about their movements each day or from season to season. Aleutian skates feed on a variety of benthic invertebrates including annelid worms, crabs, shrimp and bony fishes such as walleye pollock. Predators have yet to be identified.

USE

There are no directed fisheries for Aleutian skate in British Columbia. However, elsewhere they are encountered as bycatch, and their wings are marketed as food in Asia.

Sandpaper skate

Bathyraja kincaidii
FAMILY Arhynchobatidae (softnose skates)

CONSERVATION STATUS
Not Listed (Canada's Species at Risk Act)
Not at Risk (COSEWIC)
Data Deficient (IUCN Red List)

DESCRIPTION
The sandpaper skate is dark grey brown to black on the dorsal surface.
The dorsal surface coloration changes as the skate matures, with
juveniles having numerous dark spots on the wings and body and white
spots on either side of the tail. These spots are not evident in adults.
The ventral surface is white. The sandpaper skate is a soft-nosed skate,
with a short, broadly rounded snout. The dorsal surface is covered with

numerous prickles similar to sandpaper, which gives this species its common name. There are one or two scapular thorns on each side of the midline and a single, continuous row of median thorns from the head to the first dorsal fin. The sandpaper skate has a distinct caudal fin, separate from the second dorsal fin, and sometimes an interdorsal thorn is present.

Although it is easily confused with the Bering skate, the most useful characteristic for field identification is that the sandpaper skate possesses a continuous single row of thorns down the midline of the dorsal surface, whereas the Bering skate has a non-continuous single row of thorns with a noticeable gap between the median mid-dorsal thorns and tail thorns. Other differences between the two species are size—the sandpaper skate is the smaller of the two; shape—the sandpaper skate has a more continuous disc shape; and colour—the sandpaper skate is darker. Another historical common name for the sandpaper skate was black skate, which further added to confusion since it was an additional common name also given to the roughtail skate (*Bathyraja trachura*).

RANGE

The sandpaper skate is a common skate from northern Baja California to British Columbia. It may occur in the Gulf of Alaska, but confusion with the Bering skate makes range records difficult to confirm. It is common throughout BC waters, including the Strait of Georgia.

GENERAL BIOLOGY

The maximum total length for the sandpaper skate is 56 cm, and maximum age is estimated to be 18 years. Males and females mature at sizes of about 48 and 53 cm, respectively. These sizes correspond to approximately 11 and 13 years of age.

Sandpaper skates are oviparous and deposit egg cases on the sea floor. The egg cases are small and have distinct lateral keels (raised areas). They are rough to the touch with long horns that bend inward. It is thought that the sandpaper skate reproduces year-round, with a seasonal peak in the summer and fall. The size at hatching is 12–16 cm.

ECOLOGY

The sandpaper skate is a deepwater species, commonly found at depths between 200 and 500 m with extreme records from depths to 1,500 m. The sandpaper skate feeds on a wide variety of benthic invertebrates, ranging from krill, amphipods and annelid worms to larger prey items such as shrimp and crabs. There is no information on predators.

USE

The sandpaper skate is not used as a food fish. It is encountered in trawl and longline fisheries.

Quick Bite

Stingrays are rays that sting. They have a sharp bone located on their tail to deliver a poisonous sting when under attack.

Fine-spined skate

Bathyraja microtrachys
FAMILY Arhynchobatidae (softnose skates)

CONSERVATION STATUS
Not Listed (Canada's Species at Risk Act)
Not Assessed (COSEWIC)
 Least Concern (IUCN Red List)

DESCRIPTION

The fine-spined skate is a soft-nosed skate, with a pointed, triangular snout. It is uniformly brown on the dorsal surface with slightly darker outer disc margins. The ventral surface is white with the exception of the "wings" and the pelvic fins, which are brown. The disc is slightly wider than it is long and is covered dorsally with small prickles. The ventral surface is smooth. The fine-spined skate lacks mid-dorsal median, nuchal and scapular thorns. Adult males have well-developed alar thorns (on the dorsal surface of the pectoral fins near the tips). The tail is slightly longer than the disc, bearing a single row of well-developed median thorns and two similarly sized dorsal fins near the end. There may be a small, weakly developed interdorsal thorn. There may be a short, tapering caudal fin with a long, thin flap of skin on its upper surface.

RANGE
Distribution of this species was previously reported as occurring in the eastern north Pacific, specifically from Washington State, south to San Diego, California. Five specimens were collected in 2005 in deepwater trawling operations off the west coast of Vancouver Island from a depth of approximately 2,000 m but were only recently identified as fine-spined skates.

GENERAL BIOLOGY
Little is known about the biology of the fine-spined skate. According to recently published material, size at maturity for males is at least 64–75 cm, and 60–70 cm for females. Males grow to 75 cm. It is oviparous. Size at hatching is about 17 cm.

ECOLOGY
The fine-spined skate is a fairly common deepwater skate, living at depths of 2,000–2,900 m. They are known to feed on deepwater shrimp. Historically, this species has been confused with other deepwater skates such as the roughtail skate and the deepsea skate; however, it can be distinguished from these species by the white on its ventral surface from its snout to the pelvic region.

USE
The fine-spined skate is rarely encountered in fisheries and has no commercial value.

Quick Bite
Who are you? Skates can actually identify family members using electricity to recognize each other.

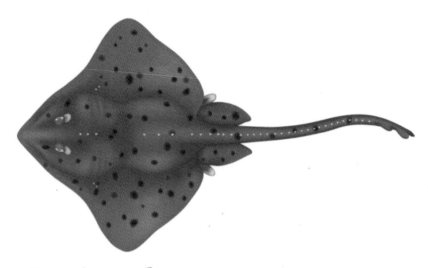

Bering skate

Bathyraja interrupta
FAMILY Arhynchobatidae (softnose skates)

CONSERVATION STATUS
Not Listed (Canada's Species at Risk Act)
Not Assessed (COSEWIC)
 Least Concern (IUCN Red List)

DESCRIPTION

The Bering skate is a soft-nosed skate, with a triangular and rounded snout tip. Dorsal coloration is dark brown to brown grey, with numerous small dark spots on the body. The snout and disc edges are usually slightly darker than the rest of the body. The ventral surface is white, usually with small to large dark-brown blotches on the underside of the tail. The disc is slightly wider than it is long and is covered dorsally in uniform, small, sandpaper-like prickles. Scapular, mid-dorsal median, and nuchal thorns are present and well developed. Adult males have a well-developed set of alar thorns. The tail is slightly longer than the disc and has a single row of non-continuous thorns and two dorsal fins, which are moderate in size and shape. A weakly developed interdorsal thorn may be present. The caudal fin is small.

Although it is easily confused with the sandpaper skate, the most useful characteristic for field identification is that the Bering skate has a non-continuous single row of thorns down the midline of the dorsal surface with a noticeable gap between the median mid-dorsal thorns and tail thorns. Other differences between the two species include size—the Bering skate is the larger of the two; shape—the Bering skate has a notched disc shape; and colour—the Bering skate is a lighter brown.

RANGE
The Bering skate is distributed throughout the eastern north Pacific from the Bering Sea and the eastern Aleutian Islands through the Gulf of Alaska south to British Columbia. Within BC waters, it is found off the west coast of Haida Gwaii and Vancouver Island as well as Queen Charlotte Sound and the Strait of Georgia.

GENERAL BIOLOGY
Maximum age estimates for the Bering skate range from 12 to 21 years for males and 13 to 21 years for females. Size at maturity for males is 69–70 cm, and 71–72 cm for females, with a maximum size of at least 89 cm. Age at maturity for both sexes is about 7 years. The Bering skate is oviparous, and size at hatching is approximately 16 cm.

ECOLOGY
This species is most common over soft bottoms on the continental-shelf-slope break at around 200–500 m deep but has been reported down to just under 1,400 m. This species was previously considered to be synonymous with the sandpaper skate, but recent unpublished molecular work has confirmed its validity as a distinct species.

USE
Although not directly targeted, the Bering skate is caught as bycatch in trawl fisheries and is used for its meat.

Roughtail skate

Bathyraja trachura
FAMILY Arhynchobatidae (softnose skates)

CONSERVATION STATUS
Not Listed (Canada's Species at Risk Act)
Not Assessed (COSEWIC)
 Least Concern (IUCN Red List)

DESCRIPTION
The roughtail skate has also been called the black skate in reference to
its coloration, which is plum brown to black on both the dorsal and
ventral surfaces. The snout is short and flexible. The roughtail skate
has no scapular or nuchal thorns, although the wings and body may
appear prickly. There is a prominent row of median thorns along the tail,
starting at the pelvic region. This row of thorns is flanked on either side

by thornlets on the tail. There are two similar-sized dorsal fins on the tail with no interdorsal thorn.

RANGE
Roughtail skates are found from the Sea of Okhotsk in the western north Pacific, throughout the Bering Sea and Aleutian Islands down to northern Baja California in the eastern north Pacific. In British Columbia, they are common from deeper waters off the west coasts of Vancouver Island and Haida Gwaii, as well as Queen Charlotte Sound and southern Hecate Strait.

GENERAL BIOLOGY
The roughtail skate can reach a maximum total length of at least 89 cm. The maximum age estimated for males is 20 years and is 17 years for females. Size at maturity is estimated to be 75 cm for both males and females.

Roughtail skates are oviparous and deposit egg cases on the sea floor. The egg cases are smooth with long and slender pointed horns that curve at the tips, sometimes crossing each other. Incubation period is unknown. The size at hatching is 9–16 cm.

ECOLOGY
The roughtail skate inhabits deep slope waters, from 200 to 2,500 m, but is usually encountered at depths greater than 600 m. The roughtail skate feeds primarily on benthic invertebrates, such as annelid worms, shrimp and crabs. As they grow larger, the roughtail skate will also eat bony fishes, such as grenadiers (family Macrouridae) and flatfish. There is no information on predators.

USE
They are known to be encountered as bycatch in deepwater trawl and longline fisheries. However, this species is not known to be used as a food fish.

Alaska skate

Bathyraja parmifera
FAMILY Arhynchobatidae (softnose skates)

CONSERVATION STATUS
Not Listed (Canada's Species at Risk Act)
Not Assessed (COSEWIC)
LC Least Concern (IUCN Red List)

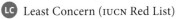
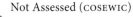

DESCRIPTION

The Alaska skate's colour ranges from brown to olive brown, with numerous dark spots on the dorsal surface. Sometimes there are two large white spots, one on each wing toward the posterior margin. The ventral surface is white. It is a soft-nosed skate, with a short and flexible snout. It has prominent scapular thorns, usually two on each side. The margins of the wings have coarse denticles from the snout to the pelvic fin insertion. The head has prominent nuchal thorns, trailed by a prominent row of median thorns that continue to the first dorsal fin. On the body, there are numerous prickles along each side of this median row of thorns.

RANGE

The full extent of the distribution of Alaska skate is unknown, but confirmed records are available from the Sea of Okhotsk in the western north Pacific, throughout the Bering Sea and Aleutian Islands and the Gulf of Alaska. In British Columbia, unconfirmed identifications report Alaska skates from waters around Haida Gwaii, including Queen Charlotte Sound, Hecate Strait and Dixon Entrance. Recently, a skate specimen from BC waters residing in the Royal BC Museum collection was confirmed as an Alaska skate.

The Alaska skate is often mistaken for the starry skate, since they look similar. The southerly extent of the Alaska skate's range and the northerly extent of the starry skate's range are unknown, and there is likely an overlap in distribution that has led to misidentification in the past.

GENERAL BIOLOGY

The maximum size of the Alaska skate is 1.1 m. The maximum observed ages for males and females are 15 years and 17 years, respectively. Age and size at maturity are 9 years and 92 cm for males and 10 years and 93 cm for females.

Alaska skates are oviparous, depositing egg cases containing a single embryo on the sea floor. The egg cases are rather smooth with some slight striations and are dark brown, with lighter brown margins. The egg cases have one set of short horns, and one set of longer horns that are flat and tapered. Embryo development exceeds 3.5 years, and the size at hatching is approximately 22 cm.

ECOLOGY

The Alaska skate is found from depths of 20–1,400 m, but is most common at 50–250 m. This species feeds primarily on bony fishes, such as Atka mackerel and walleye pollock, along with some benthic invertebrates, such as crabs and gammarid amphipods. A known predator of the Alaska skate is the Steller sea lion.

USE
This species is not used as a food fish. It is known to be incidentally encountered in trawl and longline fisheries.

Quick Bite
The modified pectoral fins of skates and rays are often called wings. This is because they gently flap these fins to "fly" through water, much like bird wings.

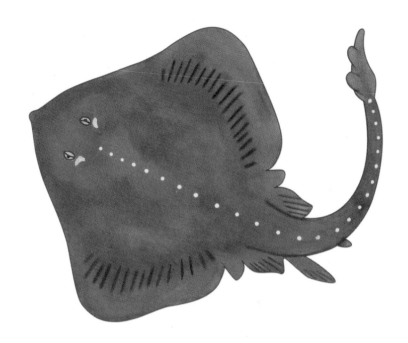

Commander skate

Bathyraja lindbergi
FAMILY Arhynchobatidae (softnose skates)

CONSERVATION STATUS
Not Listed (Canada's Species at Risk Act)
Not Assessed (COSEWIC)
 Least Concern (IUCN Red List)

DESCRIPTION
The commander skate is a soft-nosed skate, with a short, broad, flexible snout. Both surfaces are dark greyish brown. It has no scapular thorns, but there are numerous prickles along the front edge of the disc from the scapular region to pectoral fin. There are well-developed median thorns from the head extending along the length of the tail to the first dorsal fin.

RANGE

The commander skate is found from the eastern Bering Sea, through the Aleutian Islands and potentially in the western Gulf of Alaska. A single confirmed specimen has been reported off British Columbia. The skate was captured in 2009 by bottom trawl at a depth of 450 m in Queen Charlotte Sound.

GENERAL BIOLOGY

The maximum total length of the commander skate is 1 m. The maximum age of the commander skate is 35 years. Commander skates mature at approximately 21 years.

ECOLOGY

It is found from 120 to 1,200 m. It is most common below depths of 300 m.

USE

The commander skate is not used as a food fish, but small numbers are encountered as bycatch in commercial trawl and longline fisheries in Alaska.

Quick Bite

Skates and rays are designed to live on the ocean floor. They have eyes on the top of their head, with their mouth and gills on the bottom. They have a spiracle behind each eye, which helps them breathe even when they bury themselves in the sand.

Whitebrow skate

Bathyraja minispinosa
FAMILY Arhynchobatidae (softnose skates)

CONSERVATION STATUS
Not Listed (Canada's Species at Risk Act)
Not Assessed (COSEWIC)
LC Least Concern (IUCN Red List)

DESCRIPTION

The whitebrow skate has distinct white coloration around the eyes,
creating the appearance of white eyebrows. Both the dorsal and ventral
surfaces are dark brown to greyish brown. The mouth is white. The
whitebrow skate has a flexible, pointed snout that extends past the

head margin. The whitebrow skate has no scapular thorns, and there is some variation in the presence of nuchal thorns: they are often absent, but when present, they are small and few. There is a prominent row of median thorns along the tail, starting at the pelvic region.

RANGE
Whitebrow skates are found in the northeast and northwest Pacific off Japan, Russia and Alaska, and up into the Bering Sea. Off British Columbia, whitebrow skates have been captured in deepwater trawl research surveys and commercial trawl fisheries off the west coast of Haida Gwaii.

GENERAL BIOLOGY
The whitebrow skate has been estimated to live up to 35 years and can reach a maximum total length of 90 cm. Estimates of size at maturity are limited but indicate that males mature around a size of 66 cm and females around 67 cm. These sizes correspond to 23 years of age for both sexes.

Whitebrow skates are oviparous and deposit egg cases on the sea floor. The egg cases are about 7–8 cm long. Incubation period is unknown. The smallest free-swimming whitebrow skate recorded was 13 cm in total length.

ECOLOGY
Whitebrow skates inhabit deep waters on sandy gravel bottoms, from 150 to 1,400 m, but are usually encountered between 300 and 800 m. There is no information on their prey or on likely predators.

USE
This species is not known to be used as a food fish. It is encountered as bycatch in deepwater trawl and longline fisheries in Alaska.

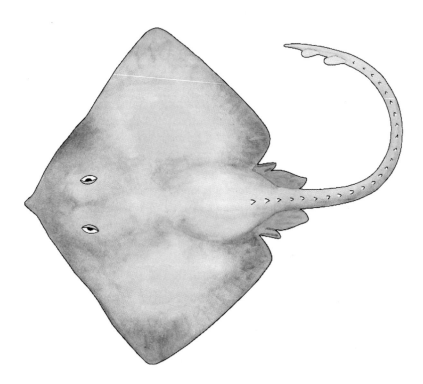

Pacific white skate

Bathyraja spinosissima
FAMILY Arhynchobatidae (softnose skates)

CONSERVATION STATUS
Not Listed (Canada's Species at Risk Act)
Not Assessed (COSEWIC)
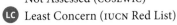 Least Concern (IUCN Red List)

DESCRIPTION
The Pacific white skate is a soft-nosed skate, with a short, flexible snout.
Both the dorsal and ventral surfaces are a pale salty grey with slightly
dusky outer margins. The disc is slightly wider than it is long and is

covered dorsally and ventrally with small prickles. Adult males have alar thorns (on the dorsal surface of the pectoral fins near the tips). The tail is slightly longer than the disc, bearing a single row of median thorns and two similar-sized dorsal fins near the end. There is no interdorsal thorn. The caudal fin is long and tapering, and has a long, thin flap of skin on its upper surface.

RANGE
Previously the Pacific white skate was known only from a few specimens found in the area from Cocos Island, Costa Rica, to Waldport, Oregon. Previous reports of this species from the Galapagos Islands may actually have been referring to records from Cocos Island. A record from the Sea of Okhotsk is now thought to be a different species. The first specimen recovered from Canada was collected in 2005 in deepwater trawling operations off the west coast of Vancouver Island from a depth of 1,950 m, but it was only recently identified as a Pacific white skate. This confirmed record extends the species range north in the eastern north Pacific Ocean over 600 km.

GENERAL BIOLOGY
Little is known about the biology of the Pacific white skate. The maximum size is at least 2 m. Maximum age and size at maturity are unknown. The Pacific white skate, like all skates, is oviparous, and size at hatching is approximately 26 cm.

ECOLOGY
The Pacific white skate is one of the deepest-living skate species. In the eastern north Pacific Ocean, it is found at depths of 800–2,900 m, generally over rocky substrates. Based on data collected by remotely operated underwater vehicle, the Monterey Bay Aquarium Research Institute has reported that the Pacific white skate is fairly abundant in its preferred habitat. It feeds on small benthic fishes.

USE
The Pacific white skate is rarely encountered and has no commercial value.

Broad skate

Amblyraja badia
FAMILY Rajidae (hardnose skates)

CONSERVATION STATUS
Not Listed (Canada's Species at Risk Act)
Not Assessed (COSEWIC)
Least Concern (IUCN Red List)

DESCRIPTION

The broad skate is brown to greyish brown with darker spots. The dorsal and ventral surfaces are similar in appearance. The pelvic fin lobes and tail are darker in colour. This species is a hardnose skate, with a short, blunt snout. The snout has several thornlets on the tip, and behind the head are two to three scapular thorns that may form a triangular pattern. There is a continuous row of median thorns along the back, from head to tail tip. This row of thorns is flanked by thornlets on the tail. The dorsal fins are similar in size with no interdorsal thorn.

RANGE

The broad skate is sporadically distributed in the eastern north Pacific from California up to the Bering Sea, and possibly westward to Japan. In Canadian waters it is found off the west coast of Vancouver Island, in Queen Charlotte Sound and off the west coast of Haida Gwaii.

GENERAL BIOLOGY

The maximum size for a broad skate is 99 cm. Males mature at a size of approximately 83 cm, but there is no information on size of maturity for females. No one has studied age in this species, and consequently, we have no estimates for age of males and females at maturity.

Broad skates are oviparous and deposit egg cases on the sea floor. However, there is no information on the size of egg cases or incubation period. Total length at hatching is estimated at 23 cm.

ECOLOGY

This species is a deepwater skate, occurring on the continental slope from approximately 850 to 2,400 m. Broad skates feed on cephalopods, crustaceans and bony fishes such as grenadiers. Predators have not been identified.

USE

This species is not known to be used as a food fish. Broad skates generally occupy depths beyond those of most fisheries, although they are infrequently encountered by deepwater trawl and trap fisheries.

Big skate

Beringraja binoculata
FAMILY Rajidae (hardnose skates)

CONSERVATION STATUS
Not Listed (Canada's Species at Risk Act)
Not at Risk (COSEWIC)
 Least Concern (IUCN Red List)

DESCRIPTION

Big skates were included in the genus *Raja* (*Raja binoculata*) until
recently, when the *Beringraja* genus was proposed for the two species
in this genus (big skate, *B. binoculata*, and mottled skate, *B. pulchra*)
that had multiple embryos per egg capsule. *B. binoculata* is currently

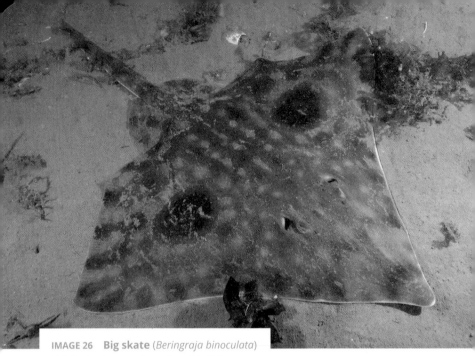

IMAGE 26 **Big skate** (*Beringraja binoculata*)
This is the largest skate found in British
Columbia, measuring over two and a half
metres. PHOTO: A. MURCH.

the accepted scientific name. As the name implies, big skates are large
bodied and are one of the larger species of skate. The big skate has a
hard, inflexible snout that is long and moderately pointed. The dorsal
surface of big skate is brown to grey, with darker mottling and prominent
eye-spots on the middle of each wing. The ventral surface is white, with
occasional darker splotches, and the pelvic fin is shallowly notched. The
big skate lacks scapular thorns and has only one nuchal thorn. There is
a continuous row of median thorns along the tail from the first dorsal
fin up to the pelvic region. The dorsal fins are the same size with an
interdorsal thorn present. The caudal fin is barely developed.

RANGE
Big skates are found from the Gulf of California to the Bering Sea. They
are very common in all waters off British Columbia.

GENERAL BIOLOGY

Big skates reach a maximum total length of over 2.5 m and have been estimated to live up to 26 years. Males and females mature at different sizes, and hence different ages. Size and age of maturity for males is estimated to be 72 cm and 6 years. Females are estimated to mature at a size of 90 cm, and at 8 years of age.

Big skates are oviparous and deposit egg cases on the sea floor. The egg cases are bright green to olive and are very large, ranging from 23 to 31 cm. The egg case has a flat ventral surface and a highly arched dorsal surface. Along the dorsal surface are very distinct parallel ridges running the full length of the egg case. The egg case has four short horns of almost equal length.

The big skate is one of only two skate species that have more than one embryo per egg case, with estimates ranging from one to eight, with three or four being most common. The embryos develop in 6–20 months depending on the water temperature. There does not appear to be a distinct breeding season, since females with fully developed egg cases are captured year-round. Northern Hecate Strait is the only identified area with high densities of egg cases. At hatching, the young range in size from 18 to 23 cm.

ECOLOGY

Big skates can be found to depths of 800 m but are most common at depths less than 200 m. They are demersal (bottom dwelling) and are considered relatively sedentary, generally not moving beyond 20 km. A few individuals may make large geographic movements, with distances of over 1,000 km recorded.

Big skates eat a variety of benthic polychaetes (bristle worms), molluscs, crustaceans and fishes. In waters off British Columbia, big skates prey on a variety of fish, including the Pacific sand lance, arrowtooth flounder, Pacific sand sole, English sole, walleye pollock, Pacific cod, buffalo sculpin and white-spotted ratfish, and invertebrates including clams, shrimp and crabs. Overall, their large size and habit of lying motionless and partly buried in soft substrates may protect them from predators. Big skates are preyed upon by large sharks such as the broadnose sevengill shark, pinnipeds such as northern elephant seals and Steller sea lions, and sperm whales.

USE

Along the entire coast of North America, big skates are encountered as bycatch in groundfish fisheries. Big skates have supported past and ongoing directed fisheries in British Columbia and the Gulf of Alaska. In British Columbia, the fisheries have landed on average about 1,000 tonnes of big skate annually. Big skates are currently managed with annual catch limits, which has reduced the targeting for big skate irrespective of international market demands. The meat from the wings is marketed for human consumption, and there is a limited market for small- to moderate-sized whole skates in Asia.

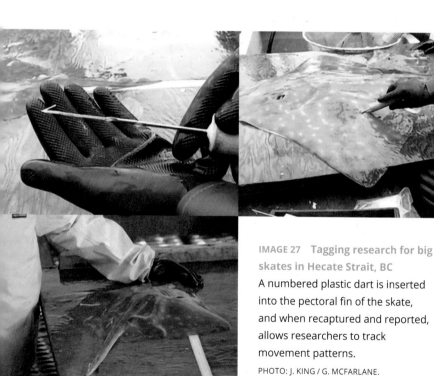

IMAGE 27 **Tagging research for big skates in Hecate Strait, BC**
A numbered plastic dart is inserted into the pectoral fin of the skate, and when recaptured and reported, allows researchers to track movement patterns.
PHOTO: J. KING / G. MCFARLANE.

Longnose skate

Raja rhina
FAMILY Rajidae (hardnose skates)

CONSERVATION STATUS
Not Listed (Canada's Species at Risk Act)
Not at Risk (COSEWIC)
 Least Concern (IUCN Red List)

DESCRIPTION

This species is another skate with a hard, inflexible snout. The longnose
skate is easily identified by its acutely pointed long nose—a characteristic
captured by the second term of its scientific name, *rhina*, derived from
the Greek *rhinos*, meaning "nose." The dorsal surface is dark brown with
faint dark and light blotches, and at the base of each pectoral fin, there
is typically an eye-spot with a pale centre. The ventral surface is bluish

grey or mottled brown to black. The pelvic fin is deeply notched. The longnose skate lacks scapular thorns, and has only one or two nuchal thorns. There is a continuous row of median thorns along the tail only. The two dorsal fins on the tail are similar in size and may have up to three interdorsal thorns. The caudal fin is barely developed.

RANGE
They are found from the Gulf of California to the Bering Sea. As with big skates, longnose skates are very common in all waters off British Columbia.

GENERAL BIOLOGY
The maximum reported length for longnose skates is 1.4 m, and they are thought to live up to 25 years. Longnose skates mature at an age of 7 years for males and 10 years for females, corresponding to 65 cm and 83 cm, respectively.

Longnose skates are oviparous, depositing their egg cases on the sea floor. The egg cases are brown, with a rough surface with a loose covering of many attachment fibres. The egg case is about 10 cm long, with single, short, hook-like horns at each corner. Each egg case contains only one embryo. Timing and frequency of egg deposits and the incubation period are not known for the longnose skate. At hatching, longnose skates are 12–17 cm long.

ECOLOGY
They are found from near the shore to depths of 1,000 m but most commonly at depths between 50 and 350 m. They are demersal (bottom dwelling) and prefer cobble habitats near rock ledges and boulders.

The primary prey for longnose skates is bony fishes. In addition, they eat shrimp and other benthic crustaceans such as crabs and bivalves. Longnose skates in turn are eaten by large elasmobranchs, cetaceans such as sperm whales, and pinnipeds (seals and sea lions). Egg cases are preyed on by molluscs, which can bore through the leathery cover and feed on the yolk inside.

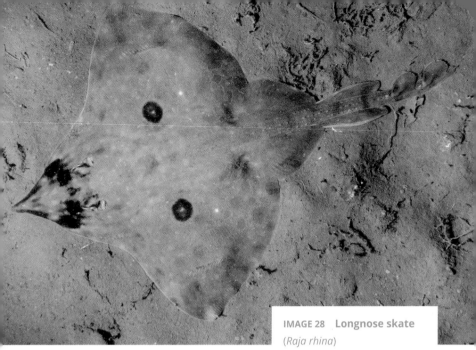

IMAGE 28 **Longnose skate**
(*Raja rhina*)
Another large skate, but distinguishable from the big skate by its elongated snout.
PHOTO: A. MURCH.

USE

Along the entire coast of North America, longnose skates are encountered as bycatch in groundfish fisheries. In British Columbia, longnose skates are caught in directed fisheries in association with big skate. They are also caught incidentally in groundfish trawl and longline fisheries that target other species. Landings are typically smaller than those for big skate and have averaged about 400 tonnes. Longnose skates are currently managed with annual catch limits. As with big skates, the meat from the wings is marketed for human consumption, and a limited market for small- to moderate-sized whole skates exists in Asia.

Starry skate

Raja stellulata
FAMILY Rajidae (hardnose skates)

CONSERVATION STATUS
Not Listed (Canada's Species at Risk Act)
Not Assessed (COSEWIC)
 Least Concern (IUCN Red List)

DESCRIPTION
The starry skate has a grey-brown dorsal surface with numerous dark spots. Black eye-spots are sometimes present mid-wing. The ventral surface is white, with a grey-brown margin. The starry skate is a hard-nosed skate, with a very short, blunt snout. The dorsal surface is covered with numerous prickles. There is a row of median thorns that begins at the base of the head and continues to the first dorsal fin. In addition, the starry skate has numerous rows of thorns on each side of the median row

of thorns, which begin at the midway body region and continue along the tail. Two similarly sized dorsal fins are present, and there may be one interdorsal thorn.

RANGE

Starry skates are found from Baja California up through southern British Columbia. The starry skate is often mistaken for the Alaska skate, since they are similar in appearance. The southerly extent of the Alaska skate and the northerly extent of the starry skate are unknown, but it is likely that both species occur in British Columbia.

GENERAL BIOLOGY

The maximum total length of the starry skate is 76 cm, and maximum age is estimated to be 11 years. Males and females mature at sizes of about 67–68 cm, which corresponds to approximately 8–9 years of age. Starry skates are oviparous and deposit egg cases on the sea floor. The egg cases are striated, and with long, prominent horns. The incubation period is unknown, and the size at hatching is 12–16 cm.

ECOLOGY

The starry skate is a nearshore skate, typically found at about 100 m, although it can be encountered at depths to 982 m, usually inhabiting rocky substrates. The starry skate feeds primarily on benthic invertebrates such as shrimp and cephalopods, and small bony fishes including small lingcod and rockfish. There is no information on predators.

USE

The starry skate is not used as a food fish. The starry skate is often found on rocky substrates, so it is rarely encountered in trawl fisheries. It is encountered in longline fisheries.

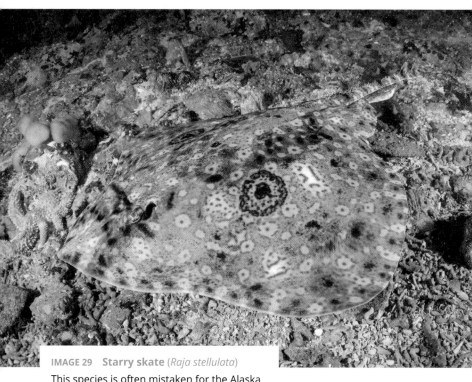

IMAGE 29 **Starry skate** (*Raja stellulata*)
This species is often mistaken for the Alaska skate (*Bathyraja parmifera*), which has confounded the definition of each species' distribution range. PHOTO: A. MURCH.

California skate

Raja inornata
FAMILY Rajidae (hardnose skates)

CONSERVATION STATUS
Not Listed (Canada's Species at Risk Act)
Not Assessed (COSEWIC)
 Least Concern (IUCN Red List)

DESCRIPTION
The California skate is a hard-nosed skate, with a moderately long and pointed snout. The dorsal surface is olive brown with occasional dark-brown mottling and distinct eye-spots. The ventral surface is lighter in colour. The dorsal surface has small scattered prickles, and the ventral surface is smooth. One to seven nuchal thorns are generally present. There are no scapular thorns. The California skate has a row of median thorns along the tail, from the pelvic region to the first dorsal fin. There is a prominent thorn between the two dorsal fins.

RANGE

The California skate is found in the Gulf of California and Baja California up to the Juan de Fuca Strait, Washington. Although there are unconfirmed reports of California skates being found in BC waters in the Juan de Fuca Strait, they have only been officially confirmed on the Washington State side. Ecologically, however, the BC side of the strait does not differ from the Washington State side, so it is most likely that the California skate occurs in BC waters as well and has yet to be reported. This would be similar to the case for Pacific angel shark, which was thought to occur in BC waters for decades before finally being photographed off Victoria.

GENERAL BIOLOGY

The maximum size is 76 cm, corresponding to a maximum age of 7 years for males and 9 years for females. Males mature at approximately 47 cm in total length; females at approximately 52 cm. California skates are oviparous. Size at hatching is 15–23 cm in total length.

ECOLOGY

It is a common nearshore species, found at depths from about 20 to 670 m. The California skate feeds on benthic invertebrates such as shrimp and annelid worms.

USE

The California skate was historically retained as a food fish when it was encountered as bycatch in commercial longline and trawl fisheries conducted in California. These landings dropped dramatically around 2007, when marine protected areas resulted in greatly reduced trawl-fishing effort. The California skate is currently a bycatch species in the hake trawl fishery operated in Mexican waters.

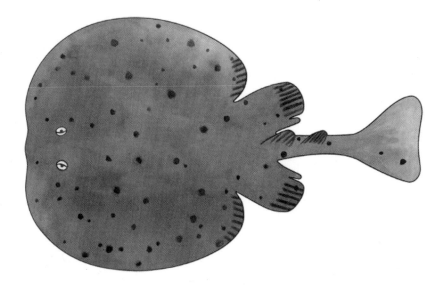

Pacific torpedo (electric) ray

Tetronarce californica

FAMILY Torpedinidae (torpedo (electric) rays)

CONSERVATION STATUS
Not Listed (Canada's Species at Risk Act)
Not Assessed (COSEWIC)
 Least Concern (IUCN Red List)

DESCRIPTION

The Pacific torpedo ray is a soft-bodied ray with a smooth dorsal surface that is dark grey to bluish or brown. The ventral surface is lighter in colour. The Pacific torpedo ray has an oval-shaped disc, with a distinct kidney-shaped electric organ on each wing, on either side of the body. The electric organs are internal, but the location of each appears lighter in colour than the rest of the dorsal surface. The first dorsal fin is twice

IMAGE 30 Pacific torpedo (electric) ray (*Tetronarce californica*)
This ray has special internal organs that produce an electric
current used to stun its prey. PHOTO: A. MURCH.

as large as the second dorsal fin. The caudal fin is large. This species has
moved between the genus *Torpedo* and the genus *Tetronarce* three times
since its discovery in 1855. The currently accepted name is *Tetronarce
californica*. This ray is also commonly called the Pacific electric ray.

RANGE
Pacific torpedo rays are found from Baja California up to northern
British Columbia. In BC waters, they are mainly encountered off the west
coast of Vancouver Island and in Queen Charlotte Sound.

GENERAL BIOLOGY
The maximum reported length for Pacific torpedo rays is 1.4 m. The
maximum age is estimated to be about 16 years. Males mature at lengths
of 65 cm and 6 years of age. Females mature at lengths of 73 cm and 9
years of age.

Unlike skates, Pacific torpedo rays are placental viviparous, giving birth to live young. The birthing season is unknown. The reproductive cycle is thought to be annual for males, and every two years for females. The gestation period is unknown. Litter sizes range from 17 to 20. At birth, Pacific torpedo rays are 18–23 cm long.

ECOLOGY

Pacific torpedo rays are found from near the shore to depths of 275 m. They are demersal (bottom dwelling) but do swim off the bottom.

Pacific torpedo rays are primarily nocturnal hunters, actively searching for prey in the mid-water near reefs and kelp beds. The electric organs produce a strong electric current used for stunning prey or predators. The primary prey is bony fishes, including pelagics such as Pacific hake, Pacific herring, anchovy and mackerel, along with flatfishes and kelp bass. They also feed on invertebrates, including cephalopods. Predators are unknown.

USE

Off California, the Pacific torpedo ray is sometimes targeted, in very low numbers, for the biomedical industry, which uses the electric organs for biomedical research. They are occasionally caught as bycatch in commercial and recreational fisheries.

Quick Bite

Pacific torpedo rays can deliver a strong electric shock of 45 volts or more to immobilize their prey or to defend themselves against attacking predators. Divers beware!

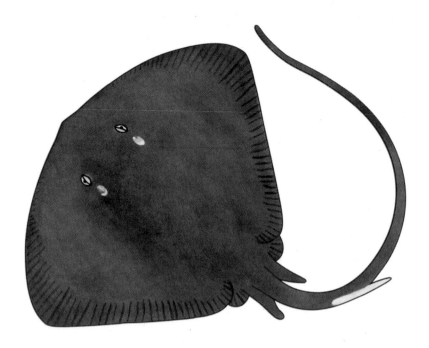

Pelagic stingray

Pteroplatytrygon violacea
FAMILY Dasyatidae (whiptail stingrays)

CONSERVATION STATUS
Not Listed (Canada's Species at Risk Act)
Not Assessed (COSEWIC)
 Least Concern (IUCN Red List)

DESCRIPTION

The pelagic stingray was originally described as *Trygon violacea* in 1832. Subsequent workers on stingray taxonomy suggested that the genus *Trygon* be synonymized with *Dasyatis* and placed the pelagic stingray in the subgenus *Pteroplatytrygon*, which was recently elevated to the rank of full genus. *Pteroplatytrygon violacea* is the current valid name for the pelagic stingray.

The pelagic stingray is characterized by a broad, wedge-shaped disc, being much wider than it is long. The whip-like tail has an extremely long stinging spine, which is potentially dangerous. The pelagic stingray lacks caudal, dorsal and pelvic fins but does have a fleshy lobe, behind the stinging spine. The dorsal and ventral surfaces are uniformly dark purple.

RANGE

In the north Pacific, the pelagic stingray is found from Baja California to southern British Columbia. There is only one confirmed record of the pelagic stingray from just outside Canadian territorial waters. A single specimen was captured in a commercial fishery in 1985, approximately 415 km off northwest Vancouver Island. There is a report of stingrays of genus *Dasyatis* encountered in the late 1920s off Kyuquot Sound (off the west coast of Vancouver Island) by salmon troll fisheries. This report likely refers to the pelagic stingray; the other member of family Dasyatidae that occurs in Pacific waters (the diamond stingray) has never been reported north of southern California, so it is unlikely that any were encountered off Kyuquot Sound.

GENERAL BIOLOGY

The pelagic stingray reaches a maximum size of 98 cm in total length. Maximum age is about 10 years, with males maturing at 2 years of age, and females at 3 years.

Reproduction is aplacental viviparous, the embryo receiving additional nutrition from the females via uterine secretions (histotrophy). The gestation period is 2–4 months. Litter size is 4–13 pups.

ECOLOGY

This species prefers open oceanic waters from the surface to at least 100 m deep, sometimes up to 230 m deep, over very deep water. The preference for oceanic waters over benthic habitat makes this species unique among stingrays. There appear to be two separate populations of pelagic stingray in the Pacific. One population occurs in the northeast and migrates between eastern equatorial waters, where birthing occurs, in winter to southern California in summer. The other

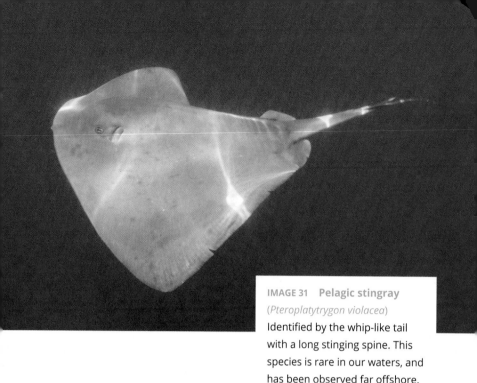

IMAGE 31 **Pelagic stingray**
(*Pteroplatytrygon violacea*)
Identified by the whip-like tail
with a long stinging spine. This
species is rare in our waters, and
has been observed far offshore.
PHOTO: A. MURCH.

population occurs in the eastern central Pacific and migrates from
warm central waters, where birthing occurs in winter, northward to
as far as Japan or possibly British Columbia in summer. They feed on
pelagic prey such as jellyfish, squids and small bony fishes. Potential
predators include sharks, such as great white sharks, and toothed
whales (dolphins, porpoises and sperm whales).

USE
The pelagic stingray has no economic value but is frequently
encountered as bycatch in commercial fisheries.

Chimeras

Order Chimaeriformes (Chimeras)

The chimeras, or ratfishes, are a small, primitive group of elongated cartilaginous fishes with soft, smooth bodies, a large head covered with sensory canals, a single gill opening and teeth fused into beak-like plates. They have large, wing-like pectoral fins, two dorsal fins and a low anal fin joined to a low caudal fin that ends in a long filamentous tail.

Most species have a large venomous dorsal fin spine. Adult males have claspers on their head and on the front of their pelvic fins to hold females during copulation. Most chimeras live in temperate ocean waters down to 2,600 m, with few species occurring at depths shallower than 200 m. The shortnose ratfishes are the exception and can be found at much shallower depths. One species of ratfish is known to occur in BC waters, but it is likely that other deepwater species may be present.

Family: Chimaeridae (shortnose chimeras)
Snout short, blunt and fleshy

Hydrolagus colliei (white-spotted ratfish)
Prominent teeth that project forward; first dorsal fin large and triangular with a long serrated spine; second dorsal fin long, low and deeply notched; anal fin joined to the caudal fin and tapering to a point; scales absent

Quick Bite

White-spotted ratfish have a spine located at the leading edge of their dorsal fin, which is used in defence. It does not present a serious danger to humans but can cause painful wounds.

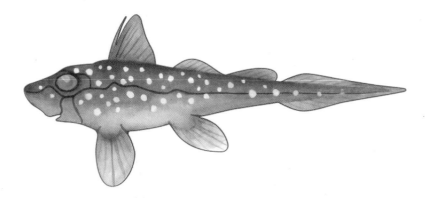

White-spotted ratfish

Hydrolagus colliei
FAMILY Chimaeridae (shortnose chimeras)

CONSERVATION STATUS
Not Listed (Canada's Species at Risk Act)
Not Assessed (COSEWIC)
LC Least Concern (IUCN Red List)

DESCRIPTION

Reminiscent of the Greek mythological creature, chimeras appear to be an odd mix of features. The name ratfish refers to their rat-like face (as well as their long rat-like tail), with prominent protruding incisor-like tooth plates. The tooth plates are ridged and fused together into three pairs. One pair protrudes from the upper jaw, and a second pair from the lower jaw. The final pair are on the upper roof of the mouth and help grind prey. Elsewhere in the world, other chimeras are known as rabbitfish, and in fact the genus for white-spotted ratfish, *Hydrolagus*, is derived from the Greek *hydro* ("water") and *lagus* ("hare" or "rabbit"). As a shortnose chimera, the white-spotted ratfish has a blunt snout. It's silvery brown with iridescent hues of gold, green and blue, and has luminescent green eyes. The dorsal surface is darker than the ventral surface. This species has numerous white spots varying in size.

The ratfish has two dorsal fins, the second of which has an undulating outline that almost divides it into two. The edges of the dorsal and caudal fins are dark, and ratfishes have a long filamentous, whip-like tail. There is a prominent dorsal spine, anterior to the first dorsal fin. The spine has a poison gland at the base, and punctures have been known to be extremely painful and result in swelling. The white-spotted ratfish has large, triangular pectoral fins that extend outward from the body and resemble airplane wings. Ratfishes are sexually dimorphic; the males have a distinct barbed, club-shaped clasper on the forehead that is likely

IMAGE 32   **White-spotted ratfish** (*Hydrolagus colliei*) A ubiquitous and abundant species in British Columbia. This species is known as a ratfish due to its long tail and prominent rodent-like teeth. PHOTO: A. MURCH.

used to grasp females during mating. Males also have pelvic claspers; however, in addition to the pair of pelvic claspers for injecting sperm, white-spotted ratfish have an extra hook-shaped pair in front of the pelvic fin for holding onto the female.

RANGE

White-spotted ratfish are distributed throughout the northeast Pacific, from southeast Alaska down through Baja California and into the Gulf of California. They are common throughout all BC waters.

GENERAL BIOLOGY

The maximum reported total length (location and sex unspecified) is 72 cm. There is a difference in observed sizes between the southern and northern ends of the white-spotted ratfish's distribution: the maximum precaudal (not including the tail) length observed in California, Washington and Oregon is 38 cm for males and 50 cm for females, and the maximum precaudal length observed in British Columbia is 67 cm for males and 69 cm for females. The maximum age estimates for white-spotted ratfish are 16 years for males and 21 years for females. There is also an increase in size of maturity with increasing latitude: off California it is approximately 29 cm (precaudal length) for males and 36 cm for females; in British Columbia it is approximately 30 cm for males and 36 cm for females. In British Columbia these sizes correspond to 12 years of age for males and 14 years for females.

The white-spotted ratfish is oviparous, with individual embryos contained in egg cases deposited onto the ocean bottom. It is estimated that females produce 19–29 egg cases each year. Incubation is estimated to be 9–12 months, and peak hatching occurs from May to October. Hatchlings emerge at about 9.6 cm long (precaudal length).

ECOLOGY

Within the northern extent of its range, white-spotted ratfish are found in bays, sounds and inland seas. It is, however, considered to be a deepwater, benthic chimera found throughout the continental shelf and slope, down to depths of 1,030 m. Aggregates of ratfish are common. There is some indication that white-spotted ratfish aggregate by size, with larger fish occupying shallower waters. This may account for the apparent sex segregation, since females are larger than males. White-spotted ratfish undergo seasonal movement into shallower waters in winter and spring and deeper waters in summer and fall. They have been observed to undergo daily movement as well, occupying deeper waters during the day and moving into shallower waters at night.

White-spotted ratfish prey on a wide variety of benthic invertebrates, including annelid worms, molluscs (such as snails, clams and squid), crustaceans (crabs and shrimp), isopods and echinoderms (such as starfish). They occasionally eat small benthic fishes. Ratfish are cannibalistic, feeding on egg cases and newly emerged hatchlings. Despite the prominent venomous dorsal spine, there are numerous predators of white-spotted ratfish. They are eaten by sharks such as sixgill, sevengill, tope and Pacific spiny dogfish; fish, including lingcod, rockfish and Pacific halibut; and marine mammals.

USE

Archaeological remains along the Pacific coast from Oregon to Alaska indicate human use of the white-spotted ratfish for millennia. First Nations on Vancouver Island are reported to have used them for food. They also extracted oil from the liver and used it internally to treat colds and sore throats, and externally to treat arthritis and earaches. It was also mixed with the black pitch of the hemlock tree and rubbed on the scalp to prevent grey hair in old age.

In the early to mid-20th century, liver oil from the white-spotted ratfish was used as a source of vitamin A and a high-quality oil for lubrication of machinery and guns. Directed reduction fisheries that caught white-spotted ratfish to grind into fish meal occurred intermittently from the mid- to late 20th century. Currently, although it is frequently encountered as bycatch in commercial fisheries, it has no economic value and is generally discarded at sea.

Glossary

Adelphophagy — Intrauterine cannibalism; the act of eating the siblings in the womb.

Aggregation — Any gathering or coming together of organisms.

Alar thorns — Rearward and downward projecting **thorns**. In male skates, a number of rows of very sharp alar thorns develop near the **lateral** margins of the **pectoral fins**. These thorns anchor the male firmly against the body and pelvic fin of the female.

Amphipods — A large group of crustaceans, most of which are small, **laterally** compressed creatures without a carapace.

Anal fin — A fin on the underside of some sharks, situated between the **pelvic fins** and the **caudal fin**.

Annelid worms — Marine **benthic** worms.

Anterior — Toward the front (head) end of the fish.

Aplacental viviparity — *See* **ovoviviparity**.

Aquaculture — The farming of aquatic organisms, including fish, molluscs, crustaceans and aquatic plants for food.

Barbels

Long whisker-like organs found near the mouths of some species. They help to locate food in poor visibility.

Batoid

A superorder of cartilaginous fishes (superorder Batoidea) containing more than 50 described species in approximately 13 families. Batoids include stingrays, skates, electric rays, guitarfishes and sawfishes.

Benthic (or **demersal**)

Referring to organisms that are bottom dwelling. Benthic sharks and skates are bottom dwellers.

Bioluminescence

Light produced by living organisms, including some sharks—for example, the lanternshark.

Bycatch

The part of a fisheries catch taken incidentally in addition to the target species. In a broad context, this includes all non-targeted fish even if those fish are landed and sold, or if they are discarded at sea.

Caudal fin

The tail fin.

Caudal keel

A ridge found on the **caudal peduncle** of some fish. It provides stability during fast movement through the water.

Caudal peduncle

The narrow part of the fish to which the tail fin is attached—the tail stalk.

Cephalofoil

The **lateral** extensions of the head in hammerhead sharks.

Chimeras	Odd relatives (subclass Holocephali) of the elasmobranchs; also known as ratfish, rabbitfish and ghost sharks.
Chondrichthyes	Cartilaginous fish, including all sharks, skates, rays and chimeras.
Citizen science	The collection and analysis of data relating to the natural world by members of the general public, typically as part of a collaborative project with professional scientists.
Claspers	The two rolls of cartilage found near the **pelvic fins** of sexually mature male sharks, skates, rays and chimeras. These serve to guide the sperm into the female's **cloaca** during mating.
Cloaca	Opening for the excretion of body waste and for reproduction.
Continental shelf	The sea bottom out from the shore to a depth of 200 metres.
Continental slope	Region of the outer edge of a continent between the generally shallow continental shelf and the deep ocean floor, from 200 to 2,000 metres; often steep and slope-like.
Cusp	A pointed structure on a tooth or **thorn**.
Cusplet	A small **cusp**.
Demersal	*See* **benthic**.

Dermal denticles   Tiny tooth-like scales on the skin of a shark. Also called placoid scales.

Directed fishery   Fishing that is directed at a certain species or group of species. This applies to both recreational and commercial fishing.

Disc   The combined head, body and enlarged **pectoral fins** of some cartilaginous fishes with compressed bodies.

Discards   The component of a fisheries catch returned to the sea, either dead or alive. Primarily made up of non-targeted, unwanted species, but can include juveniles and damaged or unsuitable individuals of the target species.

Dorsal   The upper surface or back.

Dorsal fin   The fin(s) on the upper side of the fish. Some have only one, while others have two.

Dorsoventral flattening   When an animal or plant is compressed along its dorsal (upper) and ventral (lower) side.

Ecology   A branch of biology dealing with interrelationships between organisms and their environments.

Ecosystem   Community of plants, animals and other living organisms, together with the non-living components of their environment, found in a particular habitat and interacting with each other.

Ecotourism	Travel undertaken to witness sites or regions of unique natural or ecologic quality.
Elasmobranchii	The subclass of the class Chondrichthyes (cartilaginous fishes) that sharks, rays and skates belong to.
Embryo	An earlier development stage of the young of a live-bearing shark, ranging from nearly microscopic to moderate sized but not like a miniature adult.
Euphausiids	Small, pelagic, shrimp-like crustaceans—for example, krill.
Fin spine	A small to large spine extending from the leading edge of some sharks' dorsal fins. It is a modified enamel-covered denticle.
Finning	The practice of slicing off a shark's fins and discarding the body at sea.
Fishery	An entity that raises or harvests fish. A fishery is usually described in terms of the people involved, species of fish, geographical area and fishing method.
Fusiform	Tapering toward each end; spindle shaped.
Gill	The organ that allows aquatic animals to extract oxygen dissolved in water.
Gill rakers	Stiff projections protruding from the gill arches of filter-feeders that prevent tiny food particles from passing through.

Gill slits

Most sharks have five gill slits on both sides of their heads from which water exits after being drawn in through the mouth and over the gills.

Habitat

Environment in which an organism lives. Also used to mean the environmental attributes required by a particular species, or its ecological niche.

Interdorsal spine

A spine or **thorn** on the **dorsal** surface of the fish between the first and second dorsal fins.

Isopods

A large group of small crustaceans lacking a carapace and usually having a flattened body.

Lateral

Referring to the side or directed toward the side.

Longline

Fishing gear comprising a line of considerable length bearing numerous baited hooks, and which is usually set horizontally in the water column or on the ocean bottom.

Malar thorns

Thorns found in some male skates close to the edge of the disc opposite the eye.

Nictitating eyelid

A lower movable eyelid, which protects the eye from damage, especially during feeding.

Nuchal thorns

Thorns located on the back of a skate.

Nursery ground

An area where pregnant females give birth and the young rear for a period of time.

Oophagy	When developing **embryos** feed on other eggs within the uterus.
Orbital thorns	The **thorns** around the eye.
Oviparity	A mode of reproduction where little or no embryonic development occurs inside the mother's body. Egg cases are deposited on the bottom of the ocean without further contact from the mother, and after gestation, the young emerge from the egg capsules as miniature versions of their parents.
Ovoviviparity (or aplacental viviparity)	The most common mode of reproduction among elasmobranchs, in which eggs hatch in the uterus before the embryos are fully developed, and the embryos continue to grow in the uterus without a placental connection. Nourishment is provided by the yolk sac, which is fully absorbed by the embryo before birth.
Pectoral fins	The pair of fins on either side of the body, nearest the head.
Pelagic	Relating to open water. Pelagic sharks are found free swimming in the open ocean.
Pelvic fins	The pair of fins on either side of the body, nearest the tail.
Plankton	Microscopic animals (**zooplankton**) and plants (phytoplankton) found floating in the marine environment and eaten by filter-feeders.

Population	A group of individuals of a species living in a particular area.
Predator	An animal that captures and eats other animals.
Preorbital snout length	Distance from the tip of the snout to the front of the eyeball.
Prey item	An animal taken as food by another.
Prickles	Small **dermal denticles** that can cover the entire body of some skates.
Pup	An embryonic or young shark.
Pupping	When the female shark gives birth to her young (pups).
Quota	Amount of catch or harvest allocated in a time period to a fishery as a whole or to an individual or company.
Rays	Kite- or rhomboid-shaped cartilaginous fishes occurring in subtropical and tropical marine waters throughout the world, with some species occurring in estuarine waters. Most rays are **benthic**, while some species are **pelagic**. In contrast to skates—which have fleshy tails—rays usually have slender to whip-like tails, sometimes with one or two stinging spines. Rays are also live-bearing (**viviparous**), giving rise to a relatively small number of large young.
Scapular thorns	**Thorns** located on the shoulders of a skate.

Sexual dimorphism
The condition where the two sexes of the same species exhibit different characteristics beyond the differences in their sexual organs.

Sharks
Cylindrical or flattened cartilaginous fishes with five to seven external **gill** openings on the sides of their heads, **pectoral fins** that are not attached to the head above the gill openings, and large, stout tails with large **caudal fins**. All living elasmobranchs except the **rays** or **batoids** are sharks. (Rays and skates (batoids) are essentially flattened sharks with the pectoral fins attached to their heads.) Living **chimeras** are closely related.

Skates
Bottom-dwelling, flattened, diamond-shaped cartilaginous fishes found throughout the world in temperate and polar regions, as well as in deep waters of the tropics. Unlike rays, skates are **oviparous**, depositing tough, leathery egg cases on the sea floor from which their young hatch. More than 280 species of skate have been discovered, making skates the most diverse group of all the **batoids**.

Spawning stock
The part of a stock that is mature and breeding; the number or biomass of fish beyond the age or size class in which 50 per cent of the individuals are mature.

Species
A group of interbreeding individuals with common characteristics that produce fertile (capable of reproducing) offspring and are not able to interbreed with other such groups. In other words, a population that is reproductively isolated from others.

Spiracle	A small respiratory opening behind the eye in **skates** and **rays** and some **sharks**, which directs oxygen to the eye and brain and aids water flow over the **gills**.
Squalene	Substance contained in the oil found in shark liver.
Stock	Group of individuals of a species that can be regarded as an entity for management or assessment purposes.
Sustainable fishing	Taking fewer individuals out of the population than are naturally replaced by reproduction.
Taxonomy	The classification of plants or animals according to their relations.
Teleost	Bony fish.
Thorn	A large **dermal denticle**. Although **skates** lack the stinging barbs characteristic of many **rays**, they do possess thorns that act as predator deterrents.
Thornlets	Small **thorns**.
Trawl net	A large bag-shaped fishing net that is dragged behind a boat.
Upper caudal lobe	Refers to the upper half of the **caudal fin**.
Ventral	The lower portion of **sharks** or underside of **skates** and **rays**.

Viviparity (or placental viviparity)	The most advanced mode of elasmobranch reproduction, whereby developing **embryos** in the mother are initially dependent on stored yolk but are later nourished by a direct transfer of nutrients from the mother via a yolk-sac placenta.
Warm-blooded	Able to generate its own body heat and maintain a constant temperature regardless of its surroundings.
Zooplankton	Animal plankton; animals (mostly microscopic) that drift freely in the water column.

Bibliography

Aires-da-Silva, A.M., and V.F. Gallucci. 2007. "Demographic and Risk Analyses Applied to Management and Conservation of the Blue Shark (*Prionace glauca*) in the North Atlantic Ocean." *Marine and Freshwater Research* 58(6): 570–580.

Anderson, E.D. 1980. *MSY Estimate of Pelagic Sharks in the Western North Atlantic.* Document no. 80-18, Woods Hole Laboratory, Northeast Fisheries Center. Woods Hole, MA: National Marine Fisheries Service.

Bailey, B.E., ed. 1952. *Marine Oils, with Particular Reference to Those in Canada.* Bulletin no. 89. Nanaimo, BC: Fisheries Research Board of Canada.

Baillie, J.E.M., C. Hilton-Taylor and S.N. Stuart, eds. 2004. *2004 IUCN Red List of Threatened Species: A Global Species Assessment.* Gland, Switzerland, and Cambridge, UK: IUCN Species Survival Commission. See esp. pages 21–22, "Disappearing from the Depths: Sharks on the Red-List."

Bargmann, G.G. 2009. "A History of the Fisheries for Spiny Dogfish along the Pacific Coast from California to Washington." In Gallucci, McFarlane and Bargmann, *Biology and Management of Dogfish Sharks*, 287–296.

Barraclough, W.E. 1948. "The Decline of the Tope Shark Fishery in British Columbia." In *Progress Reports*, no. 77, 91–94. Ottawa, ON: Fisheries Research Board of Canada.

Beamish, R.J., and G.A. McFarlane. 1985. "Annulus Development on the Second Dorsal Spine of the Spiny Dogfish (*Squalus acanthias*) and Its Validity for Age Determination." *Canadian Journal of Fisheries and Aquatic Sciences* 42(11): 1799–1805.

Benson, A.J., G.A. McFarlane and J.R. King. 2001. *A Phase "0" Review of Elasmobranch Biology, Fisheries, Assessment and Management.* Canadian Science Advisory Secretariat research document 2001/129. Ottawa, ON: Fisheries and Oceans Canada.

Bizzarro, J.J., A.B. Carlisle, W.D. Smith and E. Cortés. 2017. "Diet Composition and Trophic Ecology of Northeast Pacific Ocean Sharks." *Advances in Marine Biology* 77: 111–148.

Bonfil, R. 1994. *Overview of World Elasmobranch Fisheries.* Technical Paper 341. Rome, Italy: Food and Agriculture Organization of the United Nations.

———. 1999. "The Spiny Dogfish (*Squalus acanthias*) Fishery of British Columbia, Canada and Its Management." In *Case Studies of the Management of Elasmobranch Fisheries*, edited by R. Shotton, 608–655. Fisheries Technical Paper 378. Rome, Italy: Food and Agriculture Organization of the United Nations.

Bouchard, R., and D.I.D. Kennedy. 1974. *Utilization of Fishes, Beach Foods and Marine Mammals by the Tl'uhus Indian People of British Columbia.* Victoria, BC: British Columbia Indian Language Project.

Brander, K. 1981. "Disappearance of the Common Skate *Raja batis* from Irish Sea." *Nature* 290: 48–49.

Brocklesby, H.N. 1927. "Determination of Vitamin A Content in Liver Oil of the Dogfish, *Squalus suckleyi*." *Journal of Canadian Chemistry and Metallurgy* 11: 238–239.

Burde Publishing. 1921. "Shark Fishing Industry to Be Located on Alberni Canal." *Port Alberni News*, August 31, 1921.

Cailliet, G.M. 2015. "Perspectives on Elasmobranch Life-History Studies: A Focus on Age Validation and Relevance to Fishery Management." *Journal of Fish Biology* 87(6): 1271–1292.

Cailliet, G.M., and K.J. Goldman. 2004. "Age Determination and Validation in Chondrichthyan Fishes." In *Biology of Sharks and Their Relatives*, edited by J.C. Carrier, J.A. Musick and M.R. Heithaus, 399–446. Boca Raton, FL: CRC Press.

Camhi, M.D., S.V. Valenti, S.V. Fordham, S.L. Fowler and C. Gibson. 2009. *The Conservation Status of Pelagic Sharks and Rays: Report of the IUCN Shark Specialist Group Pelagic Shark Red List Workshop.* Newbury, UK: IUCN Species Survival Commission Shark Specialist Group.

Campana, S.E. 2001. "Accuracy, Precision and Quality Control in Age Determination, Including a Review of the Use and Abuse of Age Validation Methods." *Journal of Fish Biology* 59: 197–242.

Campana, S.E., F. Ferretti and A.A. Rosenberg. 2016. "Sharks and Other Elasmobranchs." Chapter 40 in *The First Global Integrated Marine Assessment: World Ocean Assessment*, edited by United Nations. Cambridge, UK: Cambridge University Press.

Campana, S.E., C. Jones, G.A. McFarlane and S. Myklevoll. 2006. "Bomb Dating and Age Validation Using the Spines of Spiny Dogfish (*Squalus acanthias*)." *Environmental Biology of Fishes* 77: 327–336.

Campbell, D., T. Battaglene and W. Shafron. 1992. "Economics of Resource Conservation in a Commercial Shark Fishery." *Australian Journal of Marine and Freshwater Research* 43(1): 251–262.

Carl, G.C. 1954. "The Hammerhead Shark in British Columbia." *Victoria Naturalist* 11(4).

Castro, J.I. 1983. *The Sharks of North American Waters*. College Station, TX: Texas A&M University Press.

Cisneros-Montemayor, A.M., M. Barnes-Mauthe, D. Al-Abdulrazzak, E. Navarro-Holm and U.R. Sumaila. 2013. "Global Economic Value of Shark Ecotourism: Implications for Conservation." *Oryx* 47(3): 381–388.

CITES (Convention on International Trade in Endangered Species of Wild Fauna and Flora). 2017. Appendices I, II and III. https://www.cites.org/eng/app/appendices.php.

Clemens, W.A., and G.V. Wilby. 1946. *Fishes of the Pacific Coast of Canada: Bulletin No. 68.* Ottawa, ON: Fisheries Research Board of Canada.

Compagno, L.J.V. 1984. *Sharks of the World: An Annotated and Illustrated Catalogue of Shark Species Known to Date.* Parts 1 and 2, FAO Fisheries Synopsis no. 125, vol. 4. Rome, Italy: Food and Agriculture Organization of the United Nations.

Cortés, E., 2000. "Life History Patterns and Correlations in Sharks." *Reviews in Fisheries Science* 8(4): 299–344.

———. 2002. "Incorporating Uncertainty into Demographic Modelling: Application to Shark Populations and Their Conservation." *Conservation Biology* 16(4): 1062–1084.

Cortés, E., F. Arocha, L. Beerkircher, F. Carvalho, A. Domingo,
M. Heupe, H. Holtzhausen, M.N. Santos, M. Ribera and
C. Simpfendorfer. 2010. "Ecological Risk Assessment of Pelagic
Sharks Caught in Atlantic Pelagic Longline Fisheries." *Aquatic Living
Resources* 23(1): 25–34.

COSEWIC. 2006. COSEWIC *Assessment and Status Report on the
White Shark* Carcharodon carcharias *(Atlantic Population, Pacific
Population) in Canada.* Ottawa, ON: Committee on the Status of
Endangered Wildlife in Canada.

——. 2007. COSEWIC *Assessment and Status Report on the Bluntnose
Sixgill Shark* Hexanchus griseus *in Canada.* Ottawa, ON: Committee
on the Status of Endangered Wildlife in Canada.

——. 2007. COSEWIC *Assessment and Status Report on the Tope*
Galeorhinus galeus *in Canada.* Ottawa, ON: Committee on the Status
of Endangered Wildlife in Canada.

Davidson, L.N.K., M.A. Krawchuk and N.K. Dulvy. 2016. "Why Have
Global Shark and Ray Landings Declined: Improved Management or
Overfishing?" *Fish and Fisheries* 17(2): 438–458.

Dulvy, N.K., J.K. Baum, S. Clarke, L.J.V. Compagno, E. Cortés,
A. Domingo, S. Fordham et al. 2008. "You Can Swim but You Can't
Hide: The Global Status and Conservation of Oceanic Pelagic Sharks
and Rays." *Aquatic Conservation: Marine and Freshwater Ecosystems*
18(5): 459–482.

Dulvy, N.K., J.D. Metcalfe, J. Glanville, M.G. Pawson and J.D. Reynolds.
2000. "Fishery Stability, Local Extinctions, and Shifts in Community
Structure in Skates." *Conservation Biology* 14(1): 283–293.

Dulvy, N.K., and J.D. Reynolds. 2002. "Predicting Extinction
Vulnerability in Skates." *Conservation Biology* 16(2): 440–450.

——. 2009. "Skates on Thin Ice." *Nature* 462: 417.

Dulvy, N.K., C.A. Simpfendorfer, L.N.K. Davidson, S.V. Fordham,
A. Brautigam, G. Sant and D.J. Welch. 2017. "Challenges and Priorities
in Shark and Ray Conservation." *Current Biology* 27(11): R565–R572.

Dunbrack, R., and R. Zielinski. 2003. "Seasonal and Diurnal Activity of
Sixgill Sharks (*Hexanchus griseus*) on a Shallow Water Reef in the
Strait of Georgia, British Columbia." *Canadian Journal of Zoology* 81:
1107–1111.

Ebert, D.A. 1986. "Biological Aspects of the Sixgill Shark, *Hexanchus griseus.*" *Copeia* 1: 131–135.

———. 2003. *Sharks, Rays and Chimaeras of California.* Berkeley, CA: University of California Press.

———. 2005. "Reproductive Biology of Skates, *Bathyraja* (Ishiyama), along the Eastern Bering Sea Continental Slope." *Journal of Fish Biology* 66(3): 618–649.

Ebert, D.A., J.S. Bigman and J.M. Lawson. 2017. "Biodiversity, Life History, and Conservation of Northeastern Pacific Chondrichthyans." *Advances in Marine Biology* 77: 9–78.

Ebert, D.A., S. Fowler and L. Compagno. 2013. *Sharks of the World: A Fully Illustrated Guide.* Plymouth, UK: Wild Nature Press.

Ferretti, F., G.C. Osio, C.J. Jenkins, A.A. Rosenberg and H.K. Lotze. 2013. "Long-Term Change in a Meso-Predator Community in Response to Prolonged and Heterogeneous Human Impact." *Scientific Reports* 3, article number 1057.

Fisheries and Oceans Canada. 2006. *Pacific Region Integrated Fisheries Management Plan: Groundfish; April 1, 2006–March 31, 2007.* Groundfish Management Unit. Vancouver, BC: Fisheries and Oceans Canada.

———. 2007. *National Plan of Action for the Conservation and Management of Sharks.* Cat. number Fs23-505/2007. Ottawa, ON: Fisheries and Oceans Canada. https://waves-vagues.dfo-mpo.gc.ca/ Library/40584306.pdf.

———. 2011. *Sharks of British Columbia.* ID guide. Cat. number Fs144-25 /2011E. Ottawa, ON: Fisheries and Oceans Canada. http://publications. gc.ca/pub?id=9.694816&sl=0.

———. 2012. *Skates of British Columbia.* ID guide. Cat. number Fs23-575/2012E. Ottawa, ON: Fisheries and Oceans Canada. http:// publications.gc.ca/pub?id=9.652451&sl=0.

———. 2016. *Evaluation of Information Available to Support the Identification of Habitat Necessary for the Survival and Recovery of Basking Shark in Canadian Pacific Waters.* Pacific region, Canadian Science Advisory Secretariat science response no. 2016/046. Ottawa, ON: Fisheries and Oceans Canada.

Food and Agriculture Organization of the United Nations. 2012. *The State of World Fisheries and Aquaculture: 2012*. Rome, Italy: Food and Agriculture Organization of the United Nations.

Friedrich, L.A., R. Jefferson and G. Glegg. 2014. "Public Perceptions of Sharks: Gathering Support for Shark Conservation." *Marine Policy* 47: 1–7.

Gallagher, A.J., P.M. Kyne and N. Hammerschlag. 2012. "Ecological Risk Assessment and Its Application to Elasmobranch Conservation and Management." *Journal of Fish Biology* 80(5): 1727–1748.

Gallucci, V.F., G.A. McFarlane and G.G. Bargmann, eds. *Biology and Management of Dogfish Sharks*. Bethesda, MD: American Fisheries Society.

Gallucci, V.F., I.G. Taylor and K. Erzini. 2006. "Conservation and Management of Exploited Shark Populations Based on Reproductive Value." *Canadian Journal of Fisheries and Aquatic Sciences* 63(4): 931–942.

Galluci, V., I. Taylor, J. King, G. McFarlane and R. McPhie. 2011. *Spiny Dogfish (Squalus acanthias) Assessment and Catch Recommendations for 2010*. Canadian Science Advisory Secretariat research document 2011/034. Ottawa, ON: Fisheries and Oceans Canada.

García, V.B., L.O. Lucifora and R.A. Myers. 2008. "The Importance of Habitat and Life History to Extinction Risk in Sharks, Skates, Rays and Chimaeras." *Proceedings of the Royal Society B: Biological Sciences* 275: 83–89.

Gertseva, V.V., and I.G. Taylor. 2012. *Status of the Spiny Dogfish Shark Resource off the Continental U.S. Pacific Coast in 2011*. Seattle, WA: National Oceanic and Atmospheric Administration.

Gillespie, G.E., and M.W. Saunders. 1994. "First Verified Record of the Shortfin Mako, *Isurus oxyrinchus*, and Second Records or Range Extensions for Three Additional Species, from British Columbia Waters." *Canadian Field-Naturalist* 108(3): 347–350.

Griffiths, A.M., D.W. Sims, S.P. Cotterell, A.E. Nagar, J.R. Ellis, A. Lynghammer, M. McHugh et al. 2010. "Molecular Markers Reveal Spatially Segregated Cryptic Species in a Critically Endangered Fish, the Common Skate (*Dipturus batis*)." *Proceedings of the Royal Society B: Biological Sciences* 277: 1497–1503.

Hamady, L.L., L.J. Natanson, G. Skomal and S. Thorrold. 2014. "Vertebral Bomb Radiocarbon Suggests Extreme Longevity in White Sharks." *PLoS ONE* 9(1): e84006. doi: 10.1371/journal.pone.0084006.

Heithaus, M.R., and L.M. Dill. 2002. "Food Availability and Tiger Shark Predation Risk Influence Bottlenose Dolphin Habitat Use." *Ecology* 83(2): 480–491.

Heithaus, M.R., A. Frid, A.J. Wirsing and B. Worm. 2008. "Predicting Ecological Consequences of Marine Top Predator Declines." *Trends in Ecology & Evolution* 23: 202–210.

Heithaus, M.R., A.J. Wirsing and L.M. Dill. 2012. "The Ecological Importance of Intact Top-Predator Populations: A Synthesis of 15 Years of Research in a Seagrass Ecosystem." *Marine and Freshwater Research* 63: 1039–1050.

Heupel, M., D.M. Knip, C.A. Simpfendorfer and N.K. Dulvy. 2014. "Sizing Up the Ecological Role of Sharks as Predators." *Marine Ecology Progress Series* 495: 291–298.

Holden, M.J. 1977. "Elasmobranchs." In *Fish Population Dynamics*, edited by J.A. Gulland, 187–215. New York, NY: Wiley and Sons.

Ketchen, K.S. 1986. *The Spiny Dogfish (Squalus acanthias) in the Northeast Pacific and a History of Its Utilization.* Canadian Special Publication of Fisheries and Aquatic Sciences, 88, catalogue no. Fs 41-31/88E. Ottawa, ON: Fisheries and Oceans.

Ketchen, K.S., N. Bourne and T.H. Butler. 1983. "History and Present Status of Fisheries for Marine Fishes and Invertebrates in the Strait of Georgia, British Columbia." *Canadian Journal of Fisheries and Aquatic Sciences* 40(7): 1095–1119.

King, J.R., and G.A. McFarlane. 2003. "Marine Fish Life History Strategies: Applications to Fishery Management." *Fisheries Management and Ecology* 10(4): 249–264.

———. 2010. "Movement Patterns and Growth Estimates of Big Skate (*Raja binoculata*) Based on Tag-Recapture Data." *Fisheries Research* 101(1): 50–59.

King, J.R., G.A. McFarlane and T.B. Zubkowski. 2018. "First Record of Commander Skate (*Bathyraja lindbergi*) in Canadian Pacific Waters." *Canadian Field-Naturalist* 132(3): 261–263. https://doi.org//10.22621/cfn.v132i3.2025.

King, J.R., and A.M. Surry. 2016. "First Record of Pacific Angel Shark (*Squatina californica*) in Canadian Pacific Waters." *Canadian Field-Naturalist* 130(4): 302–303.

———— 2017. "Seasonal and Daily Movements of the Bluntnose Sixgill Shark (*Hexanchus griseus*) in the Strait of Georgia from Satellite Tag Data." *Environmental Biology of Fishes* 100(12): 1543–1559.

King, J.R., A.M. Surry, S. Garcia and P.J. Starr. 2015. *Big Skate (*Raja binoculata*) and Longnose Skate (*R. rhina*) Stock Assessments for British Columbia.* Canadian Science Advisory Secretariat research document 2015/070. Ottawa, ON: Fisheries and Oceans Canada.

Knuckey, J.D.S. 2017. *A Taxonomic Revision of Eastern North Pacific Softnose Skates (Arhynchobatidae: Bathyraja Ishiyama).* Master's thesis, San José State University. http://scholarworks.sjsu.edu/etd_theses/4807.

Lowry, D. 2012. Management of Shark Bycatch in Washington in the Trawl and Longline Fishing Industries. In McFarlane, Arndt and Cooper, *Proceedings of the First Pacific Shark Workshop.*

Macdonald, C., A.J. Gallagher, A. Barnett, J. Brunnschweiler, D.S. Shiffman and N. Hammerschlag. 2017. "Conservation Potential of Apex Predator Tourism." *Biological Conservation* 215: 132–141.

Mackie, Q., D. Fedje, D. McLaren, N. Smith and I. McKechnie. 2011. Early Environments and Archaeology of Coastal British Columbia. In *Trekking the Shore: Changing Coastlines and the Antiquity 51 of Coastal Settlement,* edited by N.F. Bicho, J.A. Haws and L.G. Davis. New York, NY: Springer.

McFarlane, G., U.M. Arndt and E.W.T. Cooper, eds. 2012. *Proceedings of the First Pacific Shark Workshop.* December 13–15, 2011, Vancouver, BC. Vancouver, BC: World Wildlife Fund and TRAFFIC.

McFarlane, G.A., and R.J. Beamish. 1986. "A Tag Suitable for Assessing Long-Term Movements of Spiny Dogfish and Preliminary Results from Use of This Tag." *North American Journal of Fisheries Management* 6(1): 69–76.

————. 1987. "Validation of the Dorsal Spine Method of Age Determination for Spiny Dogfish." In *Age and Growth of Fish,* edited by R.C. Summerfelt and G.E. Hall, 287–300. Ames, IA: Iowa State University Press.

McFarlane, G.A., V.F. Gallucci and M.L. Miller. 2009. "Spiny Dogfish Management: Toward the Rehabilitation of an Underappreciated Species." In Gallucci, McFarlane and Bargmann, *Biology and Management of Dogfish Sharks*, 11–16.

McFarlane, G.A., and J.R. King. 2003. "Migration Patterns of Spiny Dogfish (*Squalus acanthias*) in the North Pacific Ocean." *Fisheries Bulletin* 101(2): 358–367.

———. 2006. "Age and Growth of Big Skate (*Raja binoculata*) and Longnose Skate (*Raja rhina*) in British Columbia Waters." *Fisheries Research* 78(2): 169–178.

———. 2009. "Movement Patterns of Spiny Dogfish within the Strait of Georgia." In Gallucci, McFarlane and Bargmann, *Biology and Management of Dogfish Sharks*, 77–87.

———. 2009. "Re-evaluating the Age Determination of Spiny Dogfish Using Oxytetracycline and Fish at Liberty Up to Twenty Years." In Gallucci, McFarlane and Bargmann, *Biology and Management of Dogfish Sharks*, 153–160.

McFarlane, G.A, J.R. King, K. Leask and L.B. Christensen. 2009. *Assessment of Information Used to Develop a Recovery Potential Assessment for Basking Shark* Cetorhinus maximus *(Pacific Population) in Canada.* Canadian Science Advisory Secretariat, research document 2008/071. Ottawa, ON: Fisheries and Oceans Canada.

McFarlane, G.A., R.P. McPhie and J.R. King. 2010. *Distribution and Life History Parameters of Elasmobranch Species in British Columbia Waters.* Canadian Technical Report of Fisheries and Aquatic Sciences 2908. Nanaimo, BC: Fisheries and Oceans Canada.

Mecklenburg, C.W., T.A. Mecklenburg and L.K. Thorsteinson. 2002. *Fishes of Alaska.* Bethesda, MD: American Fisheries Society.

Mumby, P.J., A.R. Harborne, J. Williams, C.V. Kappel, D.R. Brumbaugh, F. Micheli, K.E. Holmes, C.P. Dahlgren, C.B. Paris and P.G. Blackwell. 2007. "Trophic Cascade Facilitates Coral Recruitment in a Marine Reserve." PNAS *(Proceedings of the National Academy of Sciences of the United States of America)* 104(20): 8362–8367.

Musick, J.A., ed. 1999. *Life in the Slow Lane: Ecology and Conservation of Long-Lived Marine Animals*. American Fisheries Society Symposium 23. Bethesda, MD: American Fisheries Society. See esp. the introduction, "Ecology and Conservation of Long-Lived Marine Animals."

Musick, J.A., G. Burgess, G. Cailliet, M. Camhi and S. Fordham. 2000. "Management of Sharks and Their Relatives (Elasmobranchii)." *Fisheries* 25(3): 9–13.

Muter, B.A., M.L. Gore, K.S. Gledhill, C. Lamont and C. Huveneers. 2012. "Australian and U.S. News Media Portrayal of Sharks and Their Conservation." *Conservation Biology* 27(1): 187–196.

Myers, R.A., J.K. Baum, T.D. Shepherd, S.P. Powers and C.H. Peterson. 2007. "Cascading Effects of the Loss of Apex Predatory Sharks from a Coastal Ocean." *Science* 315(5820): 1846–1850.

Neff, C., and R. Hueter. 2013. "Science, Policy, and the Public Discourse of Shark 'Attack': A Proposal for Reclassifying Human–Shark Interactions." *Journal of Environmental Studies and Sciences* 3(1): 65–73.

Neff, C.L., and J.Y.H. Yang. 2013. Shark Bites and Public Attitudes: Policy Implications from the First Before and After Shark Bite Survey. *Marine Policy* 38: 545–547.

Orr, J.W., D.E. Stevenson, G. Hanke, I.B. Spies, J.A. Boutillier and G.R. Hoff. 2019. "Range Extensions and New Records from Alaska and British Columbia for the Skates *Bathyraja spinosissima* and *Bathyraja microtrachys*." *Northwestern Naturalist* 100(1): 37–47.

Orr, J.W., D.E. Stevenson, G.R. Hoff, I. Spies and J.D. McEachran. 2011. Bathyraja panthera, *a New Species of Skate (Rajidae; Arhynchobatinae) from the Western Aleutian Islands, and Resurrection of the Subgenus* Arctoraja Ishiyama. NOAA Professional Paper NMFS 11. Seattle, WA: Scientific Publications Office, National Marine Fisheries Service, National Oceanic and Atmospheric Administration.

Pardo, S.A., H.K. Kindsvater, J.D, Reynolds and N.K. Dulvy. 2016. "Maximum Intrinsic Rate of Population Increase in Sharks, Rays, and Chimaeras: The Importance of Survival to Maturity." *Canadian Journal of Fisheries and Aquatic Sciences* 73(8): 1159–1163.

Pietsch, T.W., and J.W. Orr. 2015. *Fishes of the Salish Sea: A Compilation and Distributional Analysis*. NOAA Professional Paper NMFS 18. Seattle, WA: Scientific Publications Office, National Marine Fisheries Service, National Oceanic and Atmospheric Administration.

Popular Mechanics. 1956. "Ship Spears Shark." November 1956.

Punt, A.E., and T.I. Walker. 1998. "Stock Assessment and Risk Analysis for the School Shark (*Galeorhinus galeus*) off Southern Australia." *Marine and Freshwater Research* 49: 719–731.

Robbins, W.D., M. Hisano., S.R. Connolly and J.H. Choat. 2006. "Ongoing Collapse of Coral-Reef Shark Populations." *Current Biology* 16: 2314–2319.

Saunders, M.W., and G.A. McFarlane. 1993. "Age at Maturity of the Female Spiny Dogfish (*Squalus acanthias*) in the Strait of Georgia, British Columbia, Canada." *Environmental Biology of Fishes* 38(1–3): 49–57.

Shiffman, D.S., and N. Hammerschlag. 2016. "Shark Conservation and Management Policy: A Review and Primer for Non-specialists." *Animal Conservation* 19(5): 401–412.

Simpfendorfer, C.A. 1999. "Demographic Analysis of the Dusky Shark Fishery in Southwestern Australia." In Musick, *Life in the Slow Lane*, 149–160.

Simpfendorfer, C.A., and N.K. Dulvy. 2017. "Bright Spots of Sustainable Shark Fishing." *Current Biology* 27(3): R97–R98.

Simpfendorfer, C.A., and P.M. Kyne. 2009. "Limited Potential to Recover from Overfishing Raises Concerns for Deep-Sea Sharks, Rays and Chimaeras." *Environmental Conservation* 36(2): 97–103.

Smith, J. 1946. "Harpoon Favored in Shark Fishing." *Vancouver Sun*, December 3, 1946.

Smith, S.E., D.W. Au and C. Show. 1998. "Intrinsic Rebound Potentials of 26 Species of Pacific Sharks." *Marine and Freshwater Research* 49(7): 663–678.

Southam Publishing. 1947. "Sharkhunting Latest Sport Around Texada Island." *Province* (Vancouver, BC), June 7, 1947.

Stevens, J.D., R. Bonfil, N.K. Dulvy and P. Walker. 2000. "The Effects of Fishing on Sharks, Rays and Chimaeras (Chondrichthyans) and the Implications for Marine Ecosystems." *ICES Journal of Marine Science* 57: 476–494.

Stevenson, D.E., J.W. Orr, G.R. Hoff and J.D. McEachran. 2007. *Field Guide to Sharks, Skates, and Ratfish of Alaska*. Fairbanks, AK: Alaska Sea Grant College Program, University of Alaska.

Stewart, F.L. 1975. "The Seasonal Availability of Fish Species Used by the Coast Tsimshians of Northern British Columbia." *Syesis* 8: 375–388.

Sunderland, P.A. 1937. "Gear and Bait for Grayfish and Sharks." In *Progress Reports of Pacific Biological Station, Nanaimo, B.C., and Pacific Fisheries Experimental Station, Prince Rupert, B.C.*, no. 34, released by Biological Board of Canada, 16–17. Prince Rupert, BC: Rose, Cowan & Latta.

United States Department of Interior. 1958. Alaska Fishery Statistics: 1927–1958. Washington, DC: United States Department of Interior, Fish and Wildlife Service, Bureau of Commercial Fisheries.

Victoria Daily Times. 1922. "Sharks to Yield Big Money, Says Industries Head." May 4, 1922.

Walker, T.I. 1998. "Can Shark Resources Be Harvested Sustainably? A Question Revisited with a Review of Shark Fisheries." *Marine and Freshwater Research* 49(7): 553–572.

Wallace, S., and B. Gisborne. 2006. *Basking Sharks: The Slaughter of BC's Gentle Giants*. Transmontanus, no. 14. Vancouver, BC: New Star Books.

Wallace, S., G. McFarlane, S. Campana and J.R. King. 2009. "Status of Spiny Dogfish in Atlantic and Pacific Canada." In Gallucci, McFarlane and Bargmann, *Biology and Management of Spiny Dogfish Sharks*, 313–334.

Whatmough, S., I. Van Putten and A. Chin. 2011. "From Hunters to Nature Observers: A Record of 53 Years of Diver Attitudes Towards Sharks and Rays and Marine Protected Areas." *Marine and Freshwater Research* 62(6): 755–763.

Wirsing, A.J., M.R. Heithaus and L.M. Dill. 2007. "Living on the Edge: Dugongs Prefer to Forage in Microhabitats That Allow Escape from Rather Than Avoidance of Predators." *Animal Behavior* 74(1): 93–101.

Wood, C.C., K.S. Ketchen and R.J. Beamish. 1979. "Population Dynamics of Spiny Dogfish (*Squalus acanthias*) in British Columbia Waters." *Journal of the Fisheries Research Board of Canada* 36(6): 647–656.

Worm, B., B. Davis, L. Kettemer, C.A. Ward-Paige, D. Chapman, M.R. Heithaus, S.T. Kessel and S.H. Gruber. 2013. "Global Catches, Exploitation Rates, and Rebuilding Options for Sharks." *Marine Policy* 40: 194–204.

Credits

Editing by Eve Rickert and Eva van Emden
Cover and interior design by Jeff Werner
Copy editing by Grace Yaginuma
Proofreading by Lana Okerlund
Index by Catherine Plear

Front cover photograph: Salmon shark (*Lamna ditropis*) by Andy Murch (© Andy Murch)

Map (page v) by Jeff Werner

Morphology diagrams (pages 48 and 116) and teeth diagrams by Jackie King (© Fisheries and Oceans Canada)

Species diagrams for Bering skate (page 133) and fine-spined skate (page 131) by Uko Gorter (© Uko Gorter)

Species diagrams for Pacific angel shark (page 75), commander skate (page 141), Pacific Torpedo (electric) ray (page 163), pelagic stingray (page 167), white-spotted ratfish (page 175) and lanternshark (page 71) by Jesse Woodward (© Fisheries and Oceans Canada)

All other species diagrams by Jennifer Stone (© Fisheries and Oceans Canada)

Copyright or proprietary rights for all other photographs and illustrations in this book belong to the person or organization credited in the caption.

Index

Note: Page numbers in **bold** *indicate photographs, illustrations and information found in captions.*

About the Authors

Gordon (Sandy) McFarlane spent his career as a researcher at the Pacific Biological Station in Nanaimo, British Columbia, before his retirement in 2010 and has been a scientist emeritus since. His research includes examining the climatic and oceanographic processes influencing the dynamics of marine fish, the development of ecosystem-based approaches to management, and the biology and distribution of sharks and skates off Canada's west coast. He was a member and adviser to numerous international negotiating teams and participated in the development and conduct of international research programs. He has authored more than 250 publications concerning the biology and assessment of marine resources. He lives with his wife on Vancouver Island.

Dr. Jackie King is a research scientist with Fisheries and Oceans Canada at the Pacific Biological Station in Nanaimo, British Columbia. She leads the Canadian Pacific Shark Research Program, which is responsible for research, population assessment and conservation advice for the species described in this book. She serves on international scientific committees that address the population status and conservation of sharks and their relatives. More broadly, her research focuses on how climate and ocean conditions observed throughout the north Pacific are connected to the ecosystems in BC coastal areas. Jackie lives with her family on Vancouver Island.

About the Underwater Photographer

Andy Murch is a freelance photojournalist specializing in sharks and rays. He is the CEO and expedition leader at Big Fish Expeditions and the driving force behind the Predators in Peril Project. Andy currently lives in Victoria, British Columbia, and can be contacted at info@bigfishexpeditions.com.